Data Mining
Data Warehousing

by

Ms. Khushboo Saxena
Mr. Sandeep Saxena
Dr. Akash Saxena

BPB PUBLICATIONS
B-14 Connaught Place, New Delhi-110 001

FIRST EDITION 2015

ISBN : 978-81-8333-546-1

Distributors:

COMPUTER BOOK CENTRE
12, Shrungar Shopping Centre,
M.G. Road, BENGALURU-560001
Ph: 25587923, 25584641

BPB PUBLICATIONS
B-14, Connaught Place,
NEW DELHI-110001
Ph:23325760/43526249

MICRO BOOKS
Shanti Niketan Building,
8, Camac Street, KOLKATA-700017
Ph: 22826518/22826519

BPB BOOK CENTRE
376, Old Lajpat Rai Market,
DELHI-110 006,
Ph: 23861747

MICRO MEDIA
Shop No. 5, Mahendra Chambers,
150 DN Rd. Next to Capital Cinema,
V.T. (C.S.T.) Station, MUMBAI-400 001
Ph: 22078296/22078297

INFOTECH
G-2, Sidhartha Building,
96 Nehru Place,
NEW DELHI-110 019
Ph: 26438245

DECCAN AGENCIES
4-3-329, Bank Street,
HYDERABAD-500195
Ph: 24756967/24756400

BPB PUBLICATIONS
20, Ansari Road, Darya Ganj,
NEW DELHI-110002
Ph: 23254990/23254991

Published by Manish Jain for BPB Publications, B-14, Connaught Place, New Delhi – 110001 and Printed by him at Akash press

Dedicated To

My Maternal Grand Father
Late Sri B.D. Saxena

-Khushboo Saxena

My Maternal Grand Father
Late Sri Girish Chandra Saxena

-Sandeep Saxena

My Family and friends

-Dr. Akash Saxena

Acknowledgment

No task is a single man's effort. Cooperation and Coordination of various peoples at different levels go into successful implementation of this book.

There is always a sense of gratitude, which every one expresses others for their helpful and needy services they render during difficult phases of life and to achieve the goal already set.

It is impossible to thank individually but we are here by making humble effort to thanks some of them.

At the outset we are thankful to the almighty that is constantly and invisibly guiding every body and have also helped us to work on the right path. We thank to **our parents** for their continued support to write this book. We would like to express our sincere feeling of gratitude to the Dr. **Goutam Sanyal** (Dean Academic) from NIT, Durgapur. They always motivate us to achieve high academic excellence.

We express our sense of gratitude to **Dr. Ravindra Mangal** from Maharaja Ganga Singh University, Bikaner, Rajasthan, **Dr. C.L. Saxena** Group Director TIT Bhopal, **Dr. Umesh** Director TIT Bhopal whose depth of knowledge, manner of motivation and valuable suggestions has left an everlasting image on our mind.

We are deeply indebted to Dr. Shiv Kumar, Mr. Abhishek Thoke, Mr. Rakesh Salam, Ms Deepti Sisodia, TIT Bhopal, Mr. Manish Kumar Singh, Mr. Ajeet Bhartee, Mr. Rahul Prasad, Mr. Prashant Shukla, Mr. Akhilesh Kumar Singh, Mr. Abhishek Malviya, Mr. Brajesh Kumar, Mr. Alok Kumar, Mr. Saurabh Sharma, Lucknesh Kumar GCET, Greater Noida, whose friendly suggestions and penetrating criticism has given a direction in completing this text.

We wish our thanks to all our friends and colleagues who helped and kept us motivated for writing this text. Special thanks go to

1. Dr. Shashank Srivastava , Assistant Professor, MNNIT ,Allahabad
2. Dr. Ashok Agarwal ,Associate Professor , University of Rajasthan ,Jaipur
3. Dr. Rakesh Gupta Director, SJCET, Dausa.
4. Dr. Aman Jain H.O.D ,DCTE, Jaipur
5. Dr. Rajeev Srivastava. Principal at LBS PG College, Jaipur
6. Dr. Vijay Singh Rathore Director at Shree Karni College, Jaipur
7. Dr Anurag Jain, Assistant Professor ,RITS Bhopal
8. Mr. Dinesh Goyal Vice Principal ,SGVU, Jaipur
9. Ms. Mahak Motwani, Assistant Professor, TIET Bhopal

10. Dr. Arun Sharma, H.O.D. (CSE), Mr. Surendra Kesari KIET, Ghaziabad.

11. Mr. Sunil Chauhan Associate Professor ,Jaipur

12. Mr. Sandeep Sharma, Assistant Professor, DCTE, Jaipur

13. Mr.Sansar Singh Chauhan, HOD (CS) Accurate Institute of Management & Technology, Greater Noida.

14. Mr. Mahaveer Kumar Sain, MAISM Jaipur

15. Mr.Sanjeev Pippal, JRE Greater Noida.

16. Mr.S.P.S Chauhan , Mr. Abhishekh Shivhare, ITS Greater Noida.

17. Mr. Aditya Saxena, Mr. Akhilendra Pratap Singh IIIT Allahabad

18. Ms. Shipra Saxena IIMT Engineering College greater Noida .

19. Mr. Vikas Rattan, Chitkara University.

We also thank the Publisher and the whole staff of BPB Publication, for bringing this text in a nice presentable form.

Finally, we want everyone who has directly or indirectly contributed to complete this authentic work.

Ms. Khushboo Saxena
Mr. Sandeep Saxena
Dr. Akash Saxena

Preface

The authors are confident that the present work will come as a relief to the students wishing to go through a comprehensive work explaining difficult concepts in the layman's language, offering a variety of numerical and conceptual problems along with their systematically worked out solutions and to top it, covering all the syllabi prescribed at various levels in universities.

This book promises to be a very good starting point for beginners and an asset to advanced users too.

This book is written as per the syllabus of various Technical Universities of India for the complete coverage of the syllabus for the courses of B.Tech and MCA. .Students of B.Sc. (CS), PGDCA, M.Sc. (CS) and DOEACC Society can also use this book .The content of this book are also useful for various polytechnic institutions running this subject. Difficult concepts of Data mining and warehouse are given in an easy way, so that students can able to understand in an efficient manner.

It is said "To err is human, to forgive divine". In this light we wish that the shortcomings of the book will be forgiven. At the same the authors are open to any kind of constructive criticisms and suggestions for further improvement. All intelligent suggestions are welcome and the authors will try their best to incorporate such in valuable suggestions in the subsequent editions of this book.

Ms. Khushboo Saxena
Mr. Sandeep Saxena
Dr. Akash Saxena

Table of Contents

Unit-4

Chapter 6: Introduction to Data Warehouse   72

Unit-5

Chapter 7: OLAP Technology   89

Section B

Advanced Topic on Data Mining and Warehousing   115

Unit-1

Overview, Motivation (for Data Mining),Data Mining-Definition
& Functionalities, Data Processing, Form of Data Preprocessing,
Data Cleaning: Missing Values, Noisy Data,(Binning, Clustering,
Regression, Computer and Human inspection),Inconsistent
Data, Data Integration and Transformation. Data Reduction:-
Data Cube Aggregation, Dimensionality reduction, Data
Compression, Numerosity Reduction, Clustering, Discretization
and Concept hierarchy generation.

Chapter I
Introduction to Data Mining

1.1 Overview and Definition of Data Mining

Data mining is a **non-trivial process** of discovering knowledge from huge amount
of data, as mining of gold from rocks or sand is called **gold mining**, similarly data
mining is appropriately named as knowledge mining. To extract the knowledge from
large data set **Knowledge Discovery from Data (KDD)** is used, which is discussed
in Section 1.2 in detail.

The rapid growth in computer technology is providing a great deal of development
to the databases and information industry. This is possible due to availability of a
large number of affordable data collection equipments and storage media. Therefore,
data can be stored in huge and different kinds of databases and information
repositories, which help in retrieving large volume of data and enable users to perform
sophisticated analysis.

However, an in-depth and efficient analysis becomes very difficult with such
huge amount of data which originate from various sources and are in different forms.
So, it becomes impossible for human analysts to work without use of powerful analysis
tools. As a result, decision makers make their decisions based on their intuition rather
than using the data stored in data repositories. Moreover, expert system technologies
are also totally dependable on domain experts as data in such systems are entered
manually into knowledge bases. This is time consuming, error-prone and costly
procedure. To overcome these problems, technology of data mining is used. Data

mining tools can perform various tools can perform various important functions. These tools can also discover valuable knowledge from raw data present in the Databases, Data warehouses, Web, etc. and then turn into useful information.

Data mining tasks are classified on the basis of predictive and descriptive. Prediction data mining analyzes the given dataset and basis of those behaviour predict new datasets, on the other hand descriptive data mining aims to finding such patterns which can describe the data so that they can easily understood by the humans.

1.2   Knowledge Discovery Process

Figure 1.1 shows the knowledge discovery process which comprises into some steps from raw data collections to new knowledge.

1. **Data Integration and Cleaning:** In this step, firstly combined the various data sources, and after that noise and irrelevant data must be removed from the database.

2. **Data Selection and Transformation:** In this step, analysis related data has been retrieved from the database and after that transformation would be conducted; aims to consolidate data and transforms these data into appropriate form of data processing.

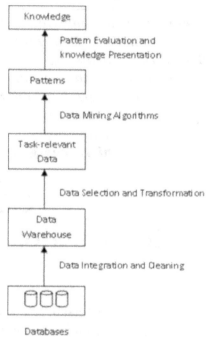

Figure 1.1: KDD Process

3. **Data Mining:** This step is concerned with the process of extracting patterns from a huge amount of data. Based on the data mining task being performed, this step applies algorithms to the transformed data to generate the desired output.

4. **Pattern Evaluation and Knowledge Presentation:** Pattern valuation identifies interesting patterns obtained in the data mining stage. To filter out discovered patterns, it may also make use of domain knowledge, such as interesting thresholds or constraints. On the other hand knowledge presentation step makes use of data visualization and knowledge techniques to present the data mining results to users.

Test Your Progress

1. Discuss the need of KDD process.
2. Explain the phases of KDD process.

1.3 Data Mining Architecture and Functionalities

Various components of data mining architecture have been shown in Figure 1.2. These components are discussed as follows:

1. **Source of Data:** This component integrates data sources which are stored in database, data warehouse, spread sheets, World Wide Web (WWW) etc. Data Selection and Data Cleaning techniques may be applied on the proposed data for further processing.

2. **Database or Data Warehouse Server:** It fetches relevant data which is based on the user's data mining request.

3. **Data Mining Engine:** This is very essential component of data mining architecture; consists of a set of functional modules to perform data mining tasks such as association, prediction, clustering, characterization, etc.

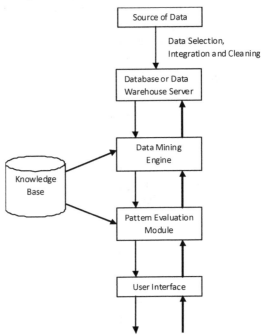

Figure 1.2: Architecture of Data Mining System

4. **Pattern Evaluation Module**: It interacts with data mining modules so as to focus the search towards interesting patterns. With the data mining module, pattern evaluation module can be merged together which depends on the implementation of the data mining method used.

5. **Knowledge Base:** It represents domain knowledge that is used to searching interesting patterns. To accomplish this concept hierarchy is being used to organize data at different level of abstractions.

6. **User Interface:** This component creates communication between users and data mining system.

Data mining functionalities and the variety of knowledge they discover are presented as Follows:

1. Classification
2. Clustering
3. Outlier analysis
4. Association

5. Data Characterization   6.   Data Discrimination

Let us discuss each of them in brief.

1. **Classification:** Classification analysis is the organization of data in given classes or in short classification is to partition the given data into predefined disjoint groups. For example,a bank loan officer wants to analyze which loan applicant are Ok and which can create risk.

2. **Clustering:** Data items are grouped according to logical relationships or customer preferences. For example, data can be mined to identify market segments or customer affinities.

3. **Outlier Analysis:** Outliers are data elements that cannot be grouped in a given class or cluster. Basically outliers are considered noise and always be removed from applications, thus this application will be very significant.

4. **Association:** Association describes relationships between a set of items that people tend to buy together.

5. **Data Characterization:** It is a summarization of the general features of data of a target class. To study the characteristics of the data which correspond to the specified class as defined by the user is done by executing anStructuredQueryLanguage (**SQL**) **query**. This means that if a user wants to know about the software products whose sales decreased by 10 percent in the last year, the only way to retrieve the data related to such products is to execute an SQL query. Several methods, such as statistical measures, data cube based OnLineAnalyticalProcessing(**OLAP**)roll-up operation, and attribute oriented induction can also be used to perform data characterization. The resulting description or output can then be presented in various forms, such as pie charts, bar charts, multi-dimensional data cubes and tables, curves, in a rule form, etc.

6. **Data Discrimination:** It is a comparison of the features of target class data objects with the features of data objects of one or more set of comparative classes. All these classes are user specified, and their data objects are retrieved by the database queries. So that if the user wants to compare general features of software products whose sales decreased by 10 percent in the last year with those whose sales increased by 10 percent during the same time, then the only way to retrieve the data related to such products is to execute an SQL query. The resulting description is presented in similar forms as those for data characterization. But it should also include comparative measures. This is because such measures help to distinguish between target and other classes.

Test Your Progress

1. Define basic architecture of data warehouse.
2. What are the functions of KDD process?

1.4   Classification of Data Mining System

Data mining systems are used to specify kind of patterns to make decision for an organization by integrate numerous technologies depending on the kinds of data to be mined. Thus to distinguish these systems on the basis of the requirements of users data mining systems classified into four types, which are described below:

1.4.1 According to Type of Data Source Mined

This type of data mining systems is categorized according to type of data handled such as, text data, World Wide Web (WWW) data, multimedia data, stream data, time series data, etc.

1.4.2 According to Data Model

This type of data mining systems are categorized according to data models used such as, relational, transactional, data warehouse, data mining or object relational system.

1.4.3 According to Data Mining Functionalities

This type of system designed for particular function such as Deoxyribonucleic acid (DNA), Stock market, fraud detection, etc. However, these applications require the integration of application specific methods on a frequent basis. Therefore all purpose data mining system might not be suitable for domain specific mining tasks.

1.4.4 According to Mining Technique Used

Data mining system provides various techniques which are classified into either user interaction level or data analysis level. Various types of advanced data mining techniques also discussed that are merits of few individual approaches.

Test Your Progress

1. Classify data mining system.
2. Which type of data mining system is not suitable for domain specific mining tasks?

1.5 Integration of Data Mining System with a Database or Data Warehouse System

Data warehouse may contain huge amount of data but this data would not be more utilized without intelligence. Thus intelligence only provided by data mining tasks which aim to discover patterns from tera byte (TB) of dataset. Hence, data mining plays an important role in data warehousing environment. To integrate data mining system to database system various integration techniques are implemented which are based on following concepts:

1. **No Coupling:** In this system database/data warehouse and data mining system is separated, means system have its own memory and storage management. This system is easy to implement by fetching the data from database and then downloaded into a data mining memory structure before applying algorithm. But this system has some problem too, first, organization of data, indexing and data searching are easy but without combining database system to data mining system task would be complex.

Second, this system is time consuming without integration of database system because database system is efficient for storing, organizing and processing data. Third, database system consist various tested and scalable algorithms which are feasible to implement, but without using these algorithms task becomes difficult for data mining systems.

2. **Loose Coupling:** This system is loosely coupled with database system, it means that data mining system has some facilities of data warehouse such as this system can only use of stored data, fetching the data and storing the mining results but cannot used for process any query on the dataset. One problem of this scheme is to high scalability and performance because data structures and query optimization methods provided by database system are not explored by loosely coupled data mining system.

3. **Partially Coupled:** In this system data mining is associated with database system, in this system some essential data mining primitives, such as sorting, indexing, analysis of histograms, pre-computation of statistical measures and pre-computation of frequently used intermediate mining results, etc. are used. As these primitives are pre-computed and are stored in data warehouse, this helps in enhancing the overall performance of a data mining system.

4. **Tight Coupling:** This system integrates with database system with whole features of data base to form one of the components of information system. In this scheme task relevant data are placed into the database system to perform all the computation after that pattern generates using data mining systems. As whole, this scheme provides efficient implementation of data mining functions, high system performance and uniform processing environment. However, implementing tight coupling scheme is non-trivial as more research needs to be done in this area.

Test Your Progress

1. How can data mining combine with database system?
2. Differentiate between Loose Coupling and Tight Coupling.

1.6   Applications of Data Mining

Various applications of data mining have been implemented such as:

1. Insurance and health care system
2. Medical / pharma
3. Retail/ marketing
4. Banking/ finance
5. Telecommunication
6. Intrusion detection
7. Market basket analysis
8. Customer segmentation and targeted marketing
9. Corporate surveillance

10. Criminal investigation and homeland security
11. Scientific enquiry and research analysis
12. Outlier detection and many more.
13. Help with decision making
14. Improve company revenue and lower costs

1.7   Issues and Challenges of Data Mining

Before data mining develops into a conventional, mature and trusted discipline, many still pending issues have to be addressed. There are several implementation issues and challenges associated with data mining, which are as follows:

1.   **Data Sources Issues:** Many types of data mining issues have been come to in mind which is related to data sources, such as diversity of data types and data glut problem.

2.   **Noisy and Irrelevant Data:** Sometimes databases can be noisy and irrelevant means some values of attributes in the database can be invalid and attributes present in the database might not be required to develop data mining task. Therefore these attributes causes difficulties in discovering relevant information out of proposed databases.

3.   **Missing Data:** In data mining process, some missing value's estimation methods are used to replace those missing values which may lead to inaccurate results.

4.   **Multimedia Data**: Data mining techniques till now proposed uses numeric, character, text data types but now-a-days new databases like **G**eographic **I**nformation **S**ystem (GIS) make use of multimedia data which can increase complexity and invalidate for many proposed algorithms.

5.   **User Interface Issues:** Technical and domain users interface can easily find out the problems which are associated with data mining tools, because technical experts aim to predict upcoming results on the other hand domain experts are useful to identifying training data and targeted results.

6.   **Interpretation of Results**: For few database users, it is not possible to correctly interpret the data mining results. Thus, technical experts are still needed for correct result interpretation.

7.   **High Dimensionality:** This refers to the problem of dimensionality curse. That is, when there are many dimensions or attributes involved in solving a data mining problem, but it is difficult to identify which one should be used. As all attributes may not be required to solve a given problem so the use of such attributes increases the overall complexity and decreases the efficiency of an algorithm.

8.   **Security and Social Issues:** Database security is a big issue of an application, in which large amounts of sensitive and private information about individuals or companies is collected and stored. This becomes controversial given the confidential nature of some of this data and the potential illegal access to the information.

9. **Mining Methodology Issues:** Versatility of mining approaches, diversity of available data, dimensionality of domain, broad analysis needs, control and handling noise, metadata, exploitation of background issues, etc., are some issues of data mining algorithms.

10. **Performance Issues:** Various algorithms like artificial intelligence and statistical methods are used for data analysis and interpretation, but these methods are not sufficient for large datasets as today raising the database. This incremental database may create issues of scalability and efficiency of data mining methods.

Test Your Progress

1. Define the limitations of data mining.
2. What are the challenges of data mining?

1.8 Data Pre-processing

Data processing is a pre-process technique of data mining, which aims to analyze the data first and if data are incomplete, missing, noisy and inconsistent it goes through various forms of data pre-processing.

1.8.1 Necessity of Pre-processing

Data quality is a big issue in the era of data mining system, for that purpose pre-processing has to be done. Data quality has to be decided by accuracy, interpretability, completeness, consistent and noiseless of data. But data may be incomplete due to non- availability of data at the time of entering data in a warehouse; data may be noise because of typing error or due to inconsistencies in naming conversations.

Timeliness is another important factor of data quality. When required data is added at the later point of time so timelines would occur to taking good decision for an organization.

Test Your Progress

1. Why is pre-processing required before data mining?
2. Name the important factor of data quality.

1.8.2 Major Tasks of Data Pre-processing

Data Cleaning: It is also known as scrubbing, aims to clean the data by fitting in missing values, removing outliers, correcting inconsistent data, smoothing noisy data. Data cleaning is a first step of pre-processing because if the data is not cleaned then mining result might be unreliable and also affects to decision making.

Sometimes various useful attribute cannot be saved in a tuple such as product customer income is called **missing value.**

Some methods to handle missing values during data cleaning has been discussed, they are:

1. **Manual entries of missing values:** In this method, missing value is filled by human. This method is not feasible and takes more time due to large data.

2. **Using attribute mean:** In this method, average value is calculated and placed for attribute whose value is missing.

3. **Using most probable value:** In this method, regression, decision tree induction, inference-based tools, are used to replace the missing value.

4. **Using global constant:** Same global constants, such as 'NA', or 'Unknown' are used to replace all missing values. Despite being simple, this method is not foolproof because replacing all the missing value with the same global value might create confusion in the mining process. That is mining program can mistakenly think that the particular attribute is of common interest as all have a value in common.

5. **Ignore the tuple:** This method is usually performed for classification, in this method; particular tuple is ignored whose class label is found to be missing.

Noise is a random error or variance in a measured variable. The various methods for smoothing the noisy data are as follows:

(i) **Binning:** This technique sorts the data values by consulting its neighbouring values then the values are divided into several buckets or called bins, where each bin represents a range of values. As binning consults its neighbouring values for smoothing a sorted data, so they are said to perform **local smoothing.**

For example, consider the data : 10,2,19,18,20,18,25,28,22

It is first sorted in the following way:

2,10,18,18,19,20,22,25,28

Now, the data are divided into bins of size 3:

Bin 1: 2,10,18

Bin 2: 18,19,20

Bin 3: 22, 25,28

Finally, the smoothing of data can be effectively done by using any of the following methods:

- Smoothing by bin means: In this method, each value in the bin is replaced by the mean value of the bin. As, the mean values of Bin 1, Bin 2 and Bin 3 are 10,19 and 25 respectively, so original values in each bin will be replaced by these mean values as follows:

  Bin 1: 10,10,10

  Bin 2: 19,19,19

  Bin 3: 25, 25,25

- Smoothing by bin medians: In this method, each value in the bin is replaced by the median of bin. If the total number of terms n is odd then median will be (n+1)/2 term and if it is even, median will be (n/2) term. In this example total number of terms is odd so median will be (3+1)/2 term which is second term of bin. Therefore, new bin will contain the following values:

  Bin 1: 10,10,10

Bin 2: 19,19,19

Bin 3: 25, 25,25

- Smoothing by bin boundaries: Here, the boundaries are the minimum and maximum values of the given bin and all the values in the bin are replaced by the closest boundary value. The larger the width of bins, the more effective is the smoothing.

Bin 1: 2,2,18

Bin 2: 18,18,20

Bin 3: 22, 22,28

(ii) **Regression:** It is a data mining technique which is used to fit an equation to a data set. That is, data get smoothened by fitting the data to a function. One of the simplest form of this technique is the linear regression which finds the best straight line to fit two attributes, such that one attribute can be used to predict the other by $Y = b + mX$. Another form of regression is multiple linear regressions which make use of more than two attributes so that complex models such as quadratic equation can be easily fitted to a multidimensional surface.

(iii) **Clustering:** In this method, each group having similar values and value which do not belong to any set of groups remain or fall outside which are considered to be outliers.

Data Integration: Data integration is an aggregation of distributed data sources (such as database, data cubes, flat files, multiple databases, etc.) in order to form a data warehouse.

Some issues in data integration are as follows:

i.   Schema integration and object matching

ii. Redundancy

iii. Detection and resolution of data value conflicts

Data Transformation: In this method, data are transformed or consolidated into forms appropriate for mining. Data transformation is done with following processes:

1. **Smoothing:** This step helps to removing noise from the data using clustering, binning and regression algorithms.

2. **Aggregation:** In this step apply aggregation operator is to applied make a data cube or for summarize the data.

3. **Generalization:** In this step, raw data are replaced by higher level concept using concept hierarchies. For example, attribute 'street' (low-level concept) can be generalized to attribute 'city' or 'country' (higher level concept).

4. **Normalization:** Itis a method to normalize attributes by scaling their values such they fall within a small specifiedand desired range; this is mostly used in classification algorithms.

5. **Feature Construction:** To improve the accuracy and better understanding of structure, feature selection method adds new attributes into a existing system. It is also helpful to discover missing information about the relationships between the data attributes which can be useful for knowledge discovery.

Data Reduction: This step is helpful to reduce the dataset from using large data set; if data is large then it will slow the data mining process. The main advantage of this technique is that even after reduction of data; integrity of original data is still maintained. Data reductions are of two typeis dimensionality reduction and numerosity reduction.

Dimensionality reduction represents the original data in the compressed or reduced form by applying data encoding or transformation on it. If the original data can be reconstructed from compressed data without losing any information, the data reduction is said to be **lossless** whereas if one can reconstruct only an approximation of the original data, the data reduction is said to be **lossy.** Two most popular techniques for dimension reduction are wavelet transform and **P**rincipal **C**omponents **A**nalysis (PCA).

Numerosity reduction method reduces the data volume by choosing alternative smaller forms of data representation.Such representation can be achieved by parametric or non-parametric method. In a parametric method, only parameters of data and outliers are stored instead of actual data whereas non-parametric methods are used to store data in reduced forms. Most popular techniques for dimension reduction are regression, long-linear models, histograms, clustering and sampling.

To implement data reduction following processes have to be used:

i. Data cube aggregation
ii. Attribute subset selection
iii. Dimensionality reduction
iv. Discretization and concept hierarchy generation

i. **Data cube aggregation:** It is a process in which information is gathered and expressed in a summarize form for various purposes, such as statistical analysis. This approach results in a data set which is smaller in volume but still maintains all the information necessary for the analysis task. For example, one needs to perform an analysis on particular item sales per year (for the years of 2012 and 2013) but the data are available on a half- yearly basis. Thus, to perform the sales yearly, the data available for the three years are aggregated as shown in Table 1.1. The aggregated information can be stored in a data cube in a multidimensional form.

For the year 2012	
Half-yearly	**Sales**
H1	600
H2	700

For the year 2013	
Half-yearly	**Sales**
H1	800
H2	600

Aggregated data for sales	
Years	**Sales**
2012	1300
2013	1400

Table 1.1: Aggregated data for sales

ii. **Attribute subset selection method:** During the analysis of data sets, many attributes may be irrelevant and redundant to the mining task which may slow down to performance of mining process. For example, if a task is to generate a list of couples who are more likely to go for a holiday package, the attributes 'marital status or age' are more relevant than the attributes 'telephone number or occupation'. Sometimes, the taste of picking up the useful attributes becomes difficult and time consuming especially when the behaviour of the data is not well known. In such situations, it is quite likely that the relevant attributes are left while irrelevant attributes are used which causes confusion for the mining algorithm employed. This result is discovery of poor quality patterns. In addition, the more the volume of irrelevant or redundant data, the slower is the missing process. To overcome such situation, a method known as attribute subset selection is employed. This method reduces the data set size and determines the minimum set of attributes by removing the irrelevant, weakly relevant or redundant attributes. The selection of attributes made such that the resulting probability distribution of data classes is almost similar to the original distribution obtained using all attributes. By doing so, it reduces the number of attributes appearing in the discovered patterns and thus helps in making patterns easier to understand. Some basic methods are used for attribute subset selections such as, stepwise forward selection method, stepwise backward elimination method, combination of forward selection and backward elimination, and decision tree induction method.

In the stepwise forward selection method, initially the reduced set is empty then the procedure iteratively determines the best attributes among all the available original attributes and adds it to the reduced set. **Stepwise backward elimination procedure** starts with the full set of attributes in the reduced set then, with each successive iteration the worst attribute is removed from the attribute set. On the other hand **combination of forward selection and backward elimination technique** with each iteration defines the best attribute from the original attributes and at the same time removes the attributes. Last technique is decision tree induction technique which we will discuss on Chapter 3

iii. **Dimensionality reduction:** It represents the original data in the compressed or reduced form by applying data encoding or transformations on it. If the original data can be reconstructed from the compressed data without losing any information, the data reduction is said to be **loseless.** On the other hand, if one can reconstruct only an approximation of the original information, the data reduction is said to be **lossy.** Wavelet transforms and principal component analysis are the two basic techniques of lossy data reduction.

iv. **Discretization and Concept hierarchy generation:** Data discretization technique divides the range of the attribute into intervals so as to reduce the number of values for a given continuous attribute. This helps in simplifying the original data because numerous values of a continuous attribute would get replaced by a small number of internal labels, thus leading to the representation of mining results in an easy to understand and concise form. On the basis of how discretization is performed, this technique is known by different names. That is , if the process first finds one or a few points to split the entire attribute range and repeat this iteratively on resulting interval, then it is called top-down discretization or splitting. On the other hand, if process considers all values of the attributes as potential points and later removes some of them by merging neighbourhood values to form intervals, then it is known as bottom-up discretization or merging. Here also the process is iteratively applied to the resulting intervals. Moreover, if the process makes use of class information, then it is known as supervised discretization else unsupervised discretization. As discretization is performed recursively on an attribute, it helps to provide a hierarchical or multi-resolution partitioning of the attribute values. This is known as concept hierarchy which in turn defines a discretization for the given attribute.

In **Short discretization** is the process of converting a continuous attribute into a discrete attribute, for example rounding off real numbers to integers whereas binarization process converting continuous/categorical attributes into one or binary attributes.

Concept hierarchy creates an attribute hierarchy which is associated with each dimension in a data warehouse. It is defined by experts or data warehouse designers which are helpful for reducing data as replacing low level concepts by higher level concepts. This hierarchy can be automatically formed for both numeric and categorical data.

Concept hierarchy generation for numeric data and categorical data is a big task for data mining process, to implement those hierarchies various methods has been discussed, these are as follows:

1. Methods for concept hierarchy generated for numeric data

   i.   **Binning:** it is a top-down splitting and unsupervised discretization technique for numerosity reduction with data smoothing.

   ii. **Histogram analysis:** It is a unsupervised discretization technique which partitions the values for an attribute into disjoint ranges called buckets. Histogram analysis algorithms are applied on each buckets until pre-specified number of concept levels has been reached.

   iii. **Entropy-based discretization:** It is a supervised discretization with its measure, such as entropy; aims to improve classification accuracy. This method determines class distribution information and split points of an attribute to form a concept hierarchy.

   iv. **ChiMerge:** It is a bottom-up approach. In this method identify best neighbouring intervals and after that they are merged and recursively creates large intervals. However, the relative class frequencies within an interval should be consistent so that discretization can be accurate. Only two adjacent intervals can be merged.

   v.   **Cluster Analysis:** The task of clustering is to group the data into a set of similar elements so that similar elements belong to the same class.

   vi. **Intuitive partitioning:** To partition the numerical ranges into easy to read uniform intervals which seem to be more intuitive or natural to users, a rule known as 3-4-5 rule is used. For example, the range of item prices 10 INR to 5000 INR within a shop is much more uniform and readable then ranges 10.560 INR to 5010.012 INR. The 3-4-5 rule partitions the given range of data into relatively equal width intervals of 3,4 or 5. This is done recursively and level-by-level on the basis of value range at the most significant digit.

2. Methods for concept hierarchy generated for categorical data

   i.   **Specifying a partial ordering of attributes explicitly at the schema level:** The concept hierarchies for categorical attributes can be defined by users or experts by specifying a partial or total ordering of attributes at the schema level. For example, if the dimension address contains a group of attributes, namely house_no, street, city, state and country, then a hierarchy can be built by specifying the total ordering among these attributes, such as house_no<street<city<country.

   ii. **Specifying a portion of a hierarchy by explicit data grouping:** This is a very effective method for large databases where it is unlikely to define an entire hierarchy by explicit value counting. In this, a portion of a concept hierarchy can be defined manually by a user. This can be done by specifying explicit groupings for a small portion of data at intermediate level. For example, if state and country from a hierarchy at schema level, then a user could normally define some intermediate levels, such as '{New minal, Shivajinagar} belongs to Bhopal' and '{Bhopal, Delhi} belongs to India'.

iii. **Specifying only a set of attributes, and not their partial ordering:** In this method, user specifies a set of attributes for forming a concept hierarchy but does not define their partial ordering. In this method, system generates the ordering of attributes automatically, so as to obtain meaningful concept hierarchy. Higher level concepts cover several lower level concepts; an attribute at high concept level will contain smaller number of mutually exclusive values in contrast with an attribute at the lower concept level. For example, the dimension 'address' has the attributes 'house_no, street, city, state and country', so the attribute 'country' has placed at the higher concept level whereas attribute 'house_no' is at lowest concept level. Once the concept hierarchy generated users/experts make some lower level swapping, wherever necessary. This heuristic rule is found to be successful in many cases.

iv. **Specifying only a partial set of attributes:** While defining a hierarchy, the user could be careless or may not have a clear idea of which attributes should be included in the hierarchy. As a result, the user might skip many attributes and include only a small subset of the relevant attributes. For example, for attribute 'address', the user may have specified only the attributes 'street' and 'city'. The formation of these partially specified hierarchies can be handled if data semantics are embedded in the database schema so that the attributes having tight semantic connections can be pinned together. By doing this, the specification of one attribute may trigger a whole group of semantically tightly linked attributes to be dragged into form a complete hierarchy.

Test Your Progress

1. What is the requirement of data reduction?
2. Why is data cleaning necessary in the KDD process?
3. What do you mean by loseless and lossy data reduction?
4. What are the methods of concept hierarchy generation for categorical dataset?

1.9 Summary

In this chapter, you have learnt about data mining. Data mining promises to generate patterns and predict behaviour of customers, products and so on which can be implemented by KDD process. Apart from its functionalities and applications, this Chapter also discussed about its limitations and how data mining system integrates with database system or data warehouse system. Data quality is an important issue in data mining which can be measured in terms of accuracy, consistency, interpretability, completeness and timeliness. Data processing has been done by various sub tasks such as data cleaning, data integration, data reduction and data transformation. Concept hierarchy is used to perform the data into multilevel of granularity. Discrcetization and binarization concepts have been discussed in this Chapter.

1.10 Key Terms

* **Clustering**: A technique in which data items are grouped according to logical relationships or customer preferences.
* **Data mining**: The computational process of discovering patterns in large datasets involving methods at the intersection of artificial intelligence.
* **KDD**: Knowledge Discovery Process.
* **Outlier analysis**: A data point which is significantly different from the remaining data.
* **SQL**: Structured Query Language; it is used to managing data supposed in a relational database management system.

1.11 Exercise

1. What is the difference between KDD and data mining?
2. Differentiate the term discretization and binarization.
3. What is data cleaning? Why it is important while building a data warehouse?
4. Explain the various strategies for data reduction.
5. How concept hierarchy is generated for numerical data?
6. What is entropy-based discretization.

University Questions

1. What is data mining?　　　**[UPTU 2007-08, 2008-09, 2009-10,2013-14]**
   Refer section 1.1
2. Identify and describe the basic phases in Knowledge Discovery from data mining.(KDD)?　　**[UPTU 2007-08,2008-09, 2010-11, 2011-12, 2012-13]**
   Refer section 1.2
3. What are the functions of data mining?　　**[UPTU 2007-08, 2011-12]**
   Refer section 1.3
4. What is data cleaning or scrubbing?　　**[UPTU 2009-10, 2010-11]**
   OR
   Explain the data cleaning.
   Refer section 1.8.2
5. Explain the Clusting and regression.　　**[UPTU 2003-04, 2009-10, Marks 5]**
   Refer section 1.3
6. What is Dimensionality Reduction?　　**[UPTU 2008-09, 2009-10, 2012-13]**
   Refer section 1.8.2

7. What is Numerosity Reduction?   **[UPTU 2009-10, 2012-13]**
    Refer section 1.8.2

8. What is the Histograms?   **[UPTU 2009-10]**
    Refer section 1.8.2

9. Identify and describe the basic phases of KDD process.   **[UPTU 2010-11]**
    OR
    Explain the data mining process with neat diagram.   **[UPTU 2009-10]**
    Refer section 1.2

10. What do you mean by cleaning of the data? Explain theimportant types of data
    cleaning.   **[UPTU 2010-11]**
    Refer section 1.8.2

11. Describe in brief process of data integration and data transformation
                                                          [UPTU 2011-12]
    Refer section 1.8.2

12. Write and describe different types of difficulties in data mining process.
                                                          [UPTU 2011-12]
    Refer section 1.7

13. Explain attribute subset selection method for data reduction with example.
                                                          [UPTU 2012-13]
    Refer section 1.8.2

14. Define the concept Hierarchies.   **[UPTU 2008-09, 2012-13,2013-14]**
    Refer section 1.8.2

Unit-2

Concept Description: Definition, Data Generalization, Analytical Characterization, Analysis of attribute relevance, Mining Class comparisions, Statistical measures in largeDatabases. Measuring Central Tendency, Measuring Dispersion of Data, Graph Displaysof Basic Statistical class Description, Mining Association Rules in Large Databases,

Association rule mining, mining Single-Dimensional Boolean Association rules fromTransactional Databases– Apriori Algorithm, Mining Multilevel Association rules fromTransaction Databases and Mining Multi-Dimensional Association rules from RelationalDatabases

Chapter 2
Concept Description

2.1   Definition

"Concept description is an automated process aims to handle complex types of concept (attributes) and their aggregation."

Concept description is a form of descriptive data mining. Basically a concept is a collection of data, such as max_sel_product, graduate_students, etc. Concept description not only calculates data; but it also provides description for characterization and comparison of the data. When a user describes concept as a class of object, it is called **class description**. **Characterization** summarizes a given data collection concisely while **comparison**provides descriptions by comparing two or more collections of data. The class discrimination or comparison mines descriptions by differentiating a target class and its contrasting classes which are comparable, that is, the classes which have similar dimensions and attributes. For example, the class, IT faculty and physics faculty are comparable but classes, age and name are not.

Test Your Progress
1.   What is concept description?

2. Explain the aim of concept description.

2.2 Data Generalization

Data generalization is a process to prepare abstracts a large set of relevant data in a database from low level concept to higher level concept. Data generalization is a form of descriptive data mining aims to provide concise data. For example, street name and landmark can be replaced by the address. This helps in summarizing the data at different levels of granularity. Today an organization has a huge amount of database and this data size is increased continuously as company growth, to manage this huge dataset (Extract, Transform, Load) ETL process is performed periodically. For that case when manager wants to view data generalized to higher levels, such as summarized data rather than examining individual employee location, then manager can easily do it if the concept of data generalization is used. It leads to class description to generate descriptions for characterization and comparison of data which is a form of data generalization. This method is also called **rolling-up data**.

There are two basic approaches for data generalization such as:

1. **Data cube approach (OnLineAnalytical Processing Approach):** In this approach computation and results are in data cube. It is very simple and efficient approach of data generalization which is helpful to make the past selling graph. To implement OLAP approach some measures would be helpful, for example count, sum, average, max whereas it deals with roll-up and drill-down operations on a data cube. These computations are performed on data cube with various levels of data abstractions. But this approach has two main limitations first, it suffers from lack of intelligence analysis and second is, only dimension of simple non-numeric data and measures of simple aggregated numeric values.

2. **Attribute Oriented Induction (AOI):** It is another technique of data generalization which was proposed in 1989 before the introduction of data cube approach. Unlike data cube approach which is essentially based on materialized view of data, AOI is an online data analysis, query oriented and generalization-based technique. In this approach, issue a database query so as to collect all tasks relevant data and after that perform generalization on the basis of different values of each attributes within the relevant data set. This generalization is done by either attribute removal or attribute generalization. Finally the identical generalized tuples are merged and their respective counts are accumulated so that aggregation can be performed. This results in a reduced generalized data set. Then this resulting generalized relation can be mapped into different forms, such as charts or rules for presenting to the users.

There are two methods of data generalization in AOI, these are:

1. **Attribute Removal:** It is based on the rule operates on large set of distinct values for an attribute in the initial working relation, but either it has no generalization operator on the attribute or higher level concepts are expressed by other attributes, so that attribute would be removed into the working relation. This is because such attribute cannot be generalized and preserving it would

lead to a large number of disjuncts. On the other hand, if the higher level concepts of an attribute are expressed in terms of other attributes, then that attribute can be removed. For example, if the higher level concepts of the attribute 'street' are represented by attributes 'city, state and country' then the attribute 'street' can be removed. It is equivalent to applying a generalization operator.

2. **Attribute generalization:** It is based on the rule operates on large set of distinct values for an attribute in the initial working relation, and applying generalization operators on the attribute, after that generalization operator must be selected and applied to the attribute.

   a. **Attribute threshold control:** This approach sets one generalization threshold for all the attributes given in large set or individual threshold for each attribute. If the number of distinct values in an attribute is greater than the specified attribute threshold, then attribute removal or attribute generalization should be carried out. Default attribute threshold ranges are from 2 to 8 but it should be varying according to user's need.

   b. **Generalized relation threshold control:** This approach sets a threshold for generalized relation. Generalization can be implementing when the number of tuples in the generalized relation is greater than the threshold value.Default attribute threshold ranges are from 10 to 30 but it should be varying according to user's need.

Test Your Progress

1. What is data generalization?
2. Explain the methods of data generalization.

2.3 Analysis of Attribute Relevance

Attribute relevance analysis is an descriptive analysis task aims to not only filter out the irrelevant or weakly relevant attributes, also retain and rank the most relevant attribute. Class characterization includes the attribute analysis is called **analytical characterization**, and if class comparison uses analysis it is called **analytical comparison.**For example, employee birth_date, birth_month, birth_year are not relevant to the employee's salary but experience is the highly relevant to the salary of employee's. Analysis of attribute relevance might be performed at multilevel abstraction and most relevant attribute included in the analysis.Attribute relevance analysis is performed as:

1. Partition the set of relevant dataset into two classes, such as target class and contrasting class.
2. Apply AOI on the dataset to perform preliminary relevance analysis by removing and generalizing attributes.
3. Calculate each attribute with selected relevance measures in the candidate relation.
4. Visit candidate relation and remove the irrelevant and weakly relevant attributes.

5. Finally generate concept description by applying AOI.

Test Your Progress

1. What is attribute relevance analysis? Explain with example.

2.4 Mining Class Comparison

Real time applications do not need to write description of single class but they need to compare two or more classes that distinguish target class to its contrasting classes. These classes are only comparable if they have similar dimensions and attributes. For example, last five years taxes are comparable but three classes, such as person, item and address are not comparable. General procedure of class comparison is:

1. Firstly select the relevant data from the dataset and partition the set of data into two classes, for example target class and another is contrasting classes.
2. Generalize both target and contrasting classes with same high-level concepts.
3. At the same high-level, compares each tuples.
4. Present description for every tupleand including two measures which are as follows:

   Support - distribution within single class.

   Comparison - distribution between classes.
5. Finally, highlight the tupleswith strong discriminantfeatures.

Test Your Progress

1. Why class comparison is is necessary into mining?
2. Describe the steps of class comparison.

2.5 Statistical Measures in Large Databases

We already discussed class description in terms of measures, such as sum, average, count, max, min and so on. These are the basic aggregate functions of relational database which are easily computed in data cube and also be used in descriptive mining of multidimensional data efficiently.

However, users want to learn more data characteristics regarding both central tendency and data dispersion, helpful to understand the distribution of data. These are discussed in Section 4.5.1 and 4.5.2 in detail.

2.5.1 Measuring Central Tendency

Central tendency measures are mean, median, mode and midrange. Let us discuss each of them in brief.

Mean: It is a center of the dataset.

Let dataset X are n values as $x_1, x_2, \ldots x_n$.

Mean of dataset X is: $X' = \frac{1}{n} \sum_{i=1}^{n} xi$

Median: Median is holistic measure means it is not a distributive measure not an algebraic measure in the sense that it computes their medians independently after that merging the medians value of each subset.Although mean function is the best way to calculating center of a dataset but for skewed data median would be most preferable. It is the middle value of ordered set if the number of values n is an odd number or if number is an even it is the average of middle two values.It is estimated by interpolation.

$$median = L_1 + (\frac{n/2 - (\sum f)l}{f_{median}})c$$

Mode: It is a most frequently occur value from a large dataset. It could be more than one, data sets with one, two or three modes are respectively called unimodal, bimodal, and trimodal whereas dataset with two or more modes is called multi-modal.

$$mean - mode = 3 \times (mean - median) \quad mean - mode = 3 \times (mean - median)$$

Empirical formula:

Midrange: It is the average of largest and smallest value of dataset.

2.5.2 Measuring Dispersion of Data

In which degree numeric data tends to spread is called **dispersion** or variance of the data. Dispersion of data includes measures, such as quartiles, outliers and variance.

Quartiles: Q1 (25th percentile), Q3 (75th percentile).

Inter-quartile range: IQR = Q3 – Q1.

Five number summary: min, Q1, M, Q3, max.

Boxplot: Ends of the box are the quartiles, median is marked, whiskers, and plot outlier individually.

Outlier: Usually, a value higher/lower than 1.5 x IQR.

Variance and standard deviation (sample: s, population: σ).

Variance: (algebraic, scalable computation).

$$s^2 = \frac{1}{n-1}\sum_{i=1}^{n}(x_i - \bar{x})^2 = \frac{1}{n-1}[\sum_{i=1}^{n}x_i^2 - \frac{1}{n}(\sum_{i=1}^{n}x_i)^2]$$

$$\sigma^2 = \frac{1}{N}\sum_{i=1}^{n}(x_i - \mu)^2 = \frac{1}{N}\sum_{i=1}^{n}x_i^2 - \mu^2$$

Standard deviation s _(or σ)_ is the square root of variance s2 _(or σ2)_.

Test Your Progress

1. Describe the measures of central tendency.
2. Explain the statistical measures of large database.

2.6   Graph Displays of Basic Statistical Class Description

Apart from pie chart, bar chart, line graph various additional graphs like histograms, scatter plots, Loess curves, quartile plots and Q-Q (Quartile-Quartile) plots has been proposed for displaying the summarized and distributions data. These graphs are briefly described as:

1. **Histograms:** It is also called frequency histograms. In this method, partitioning the data distribution of an attribute into disjoint subsets but the width of each subset should be uniform. Each subset is drawn by rectangle, whose height is equal to the count (frequency) of the subset. If an attribute is categorical data then resulting graph would be bar chart whereas if an attribute is numeric data then resulting graph called **histogram.**

2. **Scatter Plots:** This graphical method is used to determining the existence of any relationship, pattern between two numerical attributes. In this method, every pair of value considered as a pair of coordinates in an algebraic sense and plotted as points in the plane.

3. **LOESS** (Locally Estimated Scatterplot Smoothing) **Curves:** It adds a smooth curve to existing scatter plot to provide better perception of the pattern of dependence. Loess is an abbreviation for 'local regression'. To implement, itconsider two parameters, such as 'α' and 'γ' these are the smoothing and polynomials parameters. Value of α must be from ¼ to 1, which focuses on producing a fit that is usually as smooth as possible without any distortion whereas γ should be either 1 or 2. If the $\gamma=1$ means data have a gentle curvature with no local maxima and minima, and if $\gamma=2$ means that curvature is associated with local maxima and minima.

4. **Quartile Plots:** In this method, firstly data for the given attribute is displayed which allows the user to access overall behaviour and unusual occurrences of the data after that quartile information is plotted. Suppose x_i be the data stored in increasing order (i=1 to N). In this process, each x_i is paired with percentage f_i indicates the approximately $100f_i$ % of the data that are below or equal to the value x_i It is said to be approximate because there may not be a value with exactly a fraction f_i of the data below or equal to x_i The quartiles 0.25, 0.50 and 0.75 correspond to quartile Q_1, median and Q_3 respectively.

    Percentage of f_i computed as: $f_i = i-0.5/N$

5. **Q-Q (Quartile-Quartile) Plots:** In this graphical method, quartile of one univariate distribution is plotted against the corresponding quartiles of another. This provides the facility for users to view if there is any shift while moving from one distribution to another. Suppose there are two data sets $x_1, x_2,.... x_N$ and $y_1, y_2,....y_M$ for the variable salary, taken from two different branch locations, M and N. Both sets are stored in increasing order. If each set has the same number of pints, i.e., M=N then y_i is plotted against x_i where both y_i and x_i are (i-0.5)/M

quartile of their respective datasets. On the other hand, if the second branch has fewer observations than the first (i.e., M<N), then only M points can be the Q-Q plot. In this, y_i, the (i-0.5)/M quartile of y data is plotted against (i-0.5)/M quartile of x data.

Test Your Progress

1. What is histogram?
2. Differentiate Quartile plot and Q-Q plots.

2.7 Summary

In the last Chapter, it has been concluded that concept description is the most basic form of descriptive data mining, which aggregates the complex attributes. Concept or class description consists of characterization and comparison. Class comparison is also important to distinguish dataset into target class and contrasting class. Graphic user interface should be of high quality and should be highly interactive because otherwise it would be much different for business users to understand it properly.

2.8 Key Terms

- **Data generalization:** A process that abstracts a large set of task-relevant data in a database from a relatively low conceptual level to higher conceptual levels.
- **LOWESS curves**: Locally Weighted Scatterplot Smoothing; a non-parametric regression method that combine multiple regression models in a k-nearest-neighbor-based meta-model.
- **Mean**: Center of the dataset.
- **Midrange**: The average of largest and smallest value of dataset.
- **Q-Q plot**: Quantile-Quantile plot; a probability plot, which is a graphical method for comparing two probability distributions by plotting their quantiles against each other.

2.9 Exercise

1. Differentiate data generalization and summarization-based characterization.
2. Describe various measures associated with large database.
3. What is attribute-oriented induction? Also explain with an example.
4. What is data generalization?
5. Explain the method of attribute relevance analysis.
6. Why is class comparison necessary?
7. Briefly explain about quartiles, outliers, and boxplots?

How description data summarization technique is useful? Discuss some types of graphs which can be used to represent these summaries.

Chapter 3
Association Rule Mining

3.1   Introduction

In the last Chapter, you have learnt about concept hierarchy and data generalization; in this chapter you will learnt about Association rule mining, which is an application of data mining, especially in the field of marketing, retail communities, catalogue design, and other business decision-making processes. The term 'association' gives the relationship between the set of items in a particular application. Discovery of association rules is one of the major tasks of association rule mining in the data mining. For example, if a customer buys four-wheelers, there is a possibility that he/she can also buy seat cover, music system, air conditioner, etc. For that Association rule, set of items can be described as:

Four-wheeler $\Rightarrow$ seat cover, music system, air conditioner

In generalize term, association rule is described as: X Y, where $X=\{x_1, x_2.............x_n\}$ and $Y=\{y_1, y_2.............y_n\}$ are two disjoint sets, here X is called the **Antecedent** and Y is called **Consequent** of the rule. It states that if a customer tends to buy an item X, he/she is likely to buy an item Y.

For association rule to be of interest to an analyst, rule should satisfy two measures such as support and confidence. **Support** is the percentage of total transactions that satisfy antecedent and consequent of rule. If the support is low it means there is no strong evidence that the items in the itemset$(X \cup Y)$ are bought together. It is also called **prevalence.**

This is described as: support $(X \Rightarrow Y) = P(X \cup Y)$

Confidence is also called **strength**; it is the probability that a customer will buy the items in the set Y if he purchases the items in the set X. This is described as:

$$\text{Confidence } (X \Rightarrow Y) = P(Y/X) = \frac{Support(x \cup y)}{Support(x)}$$

For example, consider the large itemset L = {2,3,5} generated earlier with support_count=2. Proper non-empty subsets of L are: {2,3}, {2,5}, {3,5}, {2}, {3}, {5} with support_counts = 2,3,2,3,3,3, respectively. The association rules from these subsets are given in Table 3.1.

Table 3.1: Set of Association Rules

Association Rule A $\Rightarrow$ B	$\dfrac{Support(A \cup B)}{Support(A)}$
{2,3} $\Rightarrow$ {5}	2/2 =100%
{2,5} $\Rightarrow$ {3}	2/3=66.67%
{3,5} $\Rightarrow$ {2}	2/2= 100%
{2} $\Rightarrow$ {3,5}	2/3=66.67%
{3} $\Rightarrow$ {2,5}	2/3=66.67%
{5} $\Rightarrow$ {2,3}	2/3=66.67%

Test Your Progress

1. What is association rule mining and its necessity?
2. Explain the measures associated with association rule mining.

3.2   Market Basket Analysis

It is one of the applications of association rule mining to find associations among various items purchased by the customers. It is an efficient method to implementation of cross-selling strategies. Market basket data is a transactional process. It has three entities such as customers, purchase (basket) and items, which enables retailers to know about the frequently purchased items by customers, and thus can lead to increase in their overall sales. For example, data of customer's transactions, customer who buy a car also purchase a seat covers. Then this knowledge is helpful to promote a retailer to put a seat covers on sale at reduced price so that customers can purchase car and a set of seat covers together. This will increase the overall sale of both the items.It is defined as:

Car $\Rightarrow$ seat covers [support= 10%, confidence=60%]

3.3   Frequent Pattern Mining

Patterns that frequently appear in the dataset is called **frequent pattern** and whereas subsequence like buying two-wheeler, then helmet then gloves and if it occurs frequently in a market thus it is called **frequent sequential pattern.**

Various types of frequent patterns, correlation relationship and association rule exist. Mining of frequent patterns and rules can be classified as:

1.   On the basis of completeness of patterns to be mined

In this criteria, following patterns to be mined according to the requirement of applications. This is focussed on:

a.   **closed itemset** (if an itemset X has the same frequency of another itemset Y in a S dataset),

b.   **closed frequent itemset**(X is closed frequent item set, If X is both closed and frequent in S),

c. **maximal frequent itemset** (if X is frequent and there exists no super-itemset Y),

d. **constraint frequent itemsets** (Itemsets that satisfy a set of user-defined constraints),

e. **approximate frequent itemsets** (Itemsets that derive only approximate support counts for mined frequent itemsets),

f. **Near-match frequent item set** (Itemsets that match the support count of the near or almost matching itemsets) and

g. **Top-k frequent itemset** (Itemset that contains k items).The occurrence frequency of an itemset is the number of transactions that contain the itemset.

2. **On the basis of the levels of abstraction involved in the rule set**

It is classified according to single level and multilevel association rules. In a single level association rules given set of items does not reference items at different level of abstraction, whereas in multilevel association rules given set of items is referred at different levels of abstraction.

3. **On the basis of the number of data dimensions involved in the association rule**

It is classified as single-dimensional and multi-dimensional. In a single-dimensional rule, items or attributes refer only one dimension whereas in multi-dimensional association rules, items or attributes refer two or more dimensions.

4. **On the basis of types of values handled in the association rule**

Two types of values, such as Boolean and quantitative are handled by association rules. Boolean association rule involves associations between the presence and absence of items on the other hand quantitative association rule describes association between quantitative items or attributes.

5. **On the basis of the rules to be mined**

Frequent pattern mining can generate a various kind of rules and relationships, such as association rule, correlation rule and strong gradient relationship.

- **Association rule:**It generates a large number of relationships between itemsets.
- **Correlation rule:** If the association rule further analyzed to uncover statistical correlations.
- **Gradient:** It is the ratio of an item when compared with that of its parent, child or sibling.

Test Your Progress

1. Classify the rules of frequent pattern mining.
2. What is the aim of frequent pattern mining?

3.4   Single-Dimensional and Boolean Association Rules

If the items in an association rule are shown by only one dimension and it each item have only one value either presence or absence is called single-dimensional and Boolean association rule.

Following steps are used to implement single-dimensional association rule:

i.   Firstly prepare input dataset.

ii.   Select task relevant item set.

iii.   Evaluate support counts to find frequent item sets.

iv.   Given the frequent item sets and evaluate an association rule satisfy with the minimum confidence by computing the corresponding counts.

3.4.1 Apriori Algorithm

It is the most popular association rule algorithm. It was implemented in 1994 by R. Agrawal and R. Srikant to mining frequent itemsets for Boolean association rules.Apriori algorithm uses level-wise search strategy to explore itemsets which requires one full scan of the database. Thus, to reduce the search space and to improve the efficiency of the level-wise generation of frequent itemsets a property called **Apriori property** is used. It states that all non-empty subsets of a frequent itemset must also be frequent. It takes a database 'D' of 't' transactions and minimum support 'minsup', represented as fraction of 't', as input. Apriori algorithm generates all possible large itemsets $L_1, L_2, L_3, \ldots L_K$ as output.

The algorithm proceeds iteratively as:

Step 1: Assign the value k=1

Step 2: Generate large itemsetL_k from the set of all candidate itemsetsC_k

(a)   Scan the database D and count each itemset in C_k

(b)   If the count >minsup then

Add that itemset to L_k

Step 3: Generate candidate itemset C_{k+1} from large itemsetL_k

(a)   For k = 1, C_1 = all itemsets of length 1;

For k>1, generate C_k from L_{k-1} as follows:

- **Join Step:** C_k= k-2 way join of L_{k-1} with itself;

  If both $\{I_1, I_2, \ldots I_{k-2} I_{k-1}\}$ and $\{I_1, \ldots I_{k-2} I_k\}$ are in L_{k-1}

  Then add $\{I_1, \ldots I_{k-2} I_{k-1} I_k\}$ to C_k ;

- **Prune Step:** Remove $\{I_1, \ldots I_{k-2} I_{k-1} I_k\}$, if it does not contain a large (k-1) subset;

Step 4: increment k by 1

Step 5: Repeat steps 2,3, and 4 until C_k is empty.

In the first pass, only the sets with single items are considered for generating large itemsets. This itemset is referred to as itemset with one item. In each subsequent pass, large itemsets identified in the previous pass are extended with another item to generate larger itemsets. Therefore, the second pass considers only sets with two items, and so on. Thus by considering only the itemsets obtained by extending the large itemsets, we reduce the number of candidate large itemsets. The algorithm terminates after k passes if no large k-itemsets is found.

Example:

Database D

Transaction ID	Items
T_1	I_1, I_2, I_3, I_5
T_2	I_2, I_3, I_4, I_5
T_3	I_1, I_4, I_5
T_4	I_1, I_2, I_3, I_4, I_5

Scan Database D

C_1

Item	Count
I_1	3
I_2	3
I_3	3
I_4	3
I_5	4

Set min support as 2.

L_1

Item	Count
I_1	3
I_2	3
I_3	3
I_4	3
I_5	4

Perform $L_1 \times L_2$ to generate candidate set C_2 and repeat the process as above.

Item	Count
I_1, I_2	2
I_1, I_3	2
I_1, I_4	2
I_1, I_5	3
I_2, I_3	3
I_2, I_4	2
I_2, I_5	3
I_3, I_4	2
I_3, I_5	3
I_4, I_5	3

Calculate L_2 with predefined min support = 2.

Item	Count
I_1, I_2	2
I_1, I_3	2
I_1, I_4	2
I_1, I_5	3
I_2, I_3	3
I_2, I_4	2
I_2, I_5	3
I_3, I_4	2
I_3, I_5	3
I_4, I_5	3

$L_1 \times L_1 : C_2$ L_2

Perform $L_2 \times L_2$ to generate candidate set C_3 and repeat the process as above.

Itemset	Count
I_1, I_2, I_3	2
I_1, I_2, I_4	1
I_1, I_2, I_5	2
I_2, I_3, I_4	2
I_2, I_3, I_5	3
I_3, I_4, I_5	2

Calculate L_3 with predefined min support = 2.

Item	Count
I_1, I_2, I_3	2
I_1, I_2, I_5	2
I_2, I_3, I_4	2
I_2, I_3, I_5	2
I_3, I_4, I_5	2

$$L_2 \times L_2 : C_3$$ $$L_3$$

Perform $L_3 \times L_3$ to generate candidate set C_4 and repeat the process as above.

Item	Count
I_1, I_2, I_3, I_5	2
I_2, I_3, I_4, I_5	2
I_3, I_4, I_5, I_1	1
I_1, I_2, I_3, I_4	1

Calculate L_4 with predefined min support as 2.

Item	Count
I_1, I_2, I_3, I_4	1
I_1, I_2, I_3, I_5	2
I_2, I_3, I_4, I_5	2
I_3, I_4, I_5, I_1	1

Now more pair will be made with minimum support, so have we an see that frequent Item sets in a database are

I_1, I_2, I_3, I_5

I_2, I_3, I_4, I_5

Test Your Progress

1. Explain the basic steps of single-dimensional association rules.
2. Describe Apriori algorithm.

3.4.2 Improving the Efficiency of Apriori Algorithm

This section discusses about the modification in Apriori algorithm in the context of computational complexity. Some improvements are:

1. **Hashing:** An itemset is not frequent if, Hashing bucket count of those itemset is below to the threshold.

2. **Transaction Reduction**: Aim of this technique is to reduce the number of transactions in future that do not have any frequent itemset.

3. **Data Set Partitioning**: In this technique, data or a set of transactions is partitioned into smaller segments for the purpose of finding candidate itemsets.

4. **Sampling:** This technique is important when efficiency is most important than accuracy. It is based on the mining on a subset of the given data.

5. **Dynamic Itemset Counting:** In this technique during scanning, candidate itemset would be added at different start point, if all their subsets are estimated.

Although above improvements were used to improve the efficiency of Apriori algorithm, reduce the size of candidate itemsets and lead to good performance gain, still they have two limitations. These are as follows:

1. Difficult to handle a large number of itemsets.For example if there are 10^4 frequent 1-itemset, then approximately 10^7 candidate 2-itemsets are generated. Moreover, if there is a frequent itemset of size 100, then approximately 10^{30} candidate itemsets are generated in this process.

2. It is tedious to repeatedly scan the database and check a large set of candidates by pattern matching. It is also difficult to go over each transaction in the database to determine the support of the candidate itemsets.

3.4.3 Mining Frequent Patterns without Candidate Generation: FP-Growth

This algorithm was proposed by Han et al, to mine the complete set of frequent itemsets and avoid the generation of large number of candidates sets is **Frequent-Pattern (FP) growth**. It creates **FP tree** to compress a large database. In this tree nodes, frequent items are arranged in such a manner that more frequently occurring nodes have better chances of sharing nodes than the less frequently occurring ones. This algorithm uses divide and conquer method to decompose mining task after that avoid candidate generation by consider sub-database only. FP growth algorithm preserves whole information for frequent pattern mining. It has some **advantages,**such as it scans the database only twice which helps in decreasing computation cost, second, it uses divide and conquer method so the size of subsequent conditional FP-tree is reduced. Apart from this FP-growth algorithm has some **disadvantages,** such as it is difficult to be used in an interactive mining process as users may change the support threshold according to the rules which may lead to repetition of the whole mining process. Second, It is not suitable for incremental mining.

FP-growth algorithm is as follows:

1. **Construct conditional pattern base for each node in the FP-tree.**
    (a) Starting at the frequent header table in the FP-tree.
    (b) Traverse the FP-tree by following the link of each frequent item.
    (c) Accumulate all of transformed prefix paths of that item to form a conditional pattern base.

2. **Construct conditional FP-tree from each conditional pattern-base.**
    (a) Accumulate the count for each item in the base.
    (b) Construct the FP-tree for the frequent items of the pattern base.

3. **Recursively mine conditional FP-trees and grow frequent patterns obtained so far.**
    *   If the conditional FP-tree contains a single path, simply enumerate all the patterns.

FP-Growth Example

Database D

Transaction ID	Item
T_1	I_1, I_2, I_3, I_5
T_2	I_2, I_3, I_4, I_5
T_3	I_1, I_4, I_5
T_4	I_1, I_2, I_3, I_4, I_5

Scan Database ⟶

Item	Count
I_1	3
I_2	3
I_3	3
I_4	3
I_5	5

After that, all the itemset arrange in a sequential order or give the priority, and construct FP-tree. And new conside, the items as a suffix for the database D and arrange the items or Transaction according to priority.

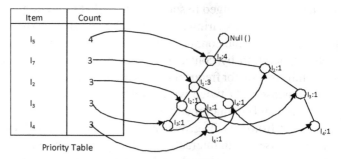

Item	Count
I_5	4
I_7	3
I_2	3
I_3	3
I_4	3

Priority Table

After that FP-tree of priority table, insert this priority tabel except item I_5 because it contains higher priority and mining the above FP-tree as summarised in Table 3.2.

Table 3.2 FP-Tree of Priority Table

Item	Conditional Pattern Base FP-tree	Conditional Generated	Frequent Pattern
I_4	$(I_1, I_2, I_3 : 1), (I_2, I_3 : 1),$ $(I_1 : 1)$	$(I_2, I_3 : 2),$ $(I_1 : 2)$	$(I_2, I_3, I_4 : 1)$ $(I_1, I_4 : 2)$
I_3	$(I_1, I_2 : 2) (I_2 : 1)$	$(I_1, I_2 : 2), (I_2 : 3)$	$(I_1, I_2, I_3 : 3)$ $(I_2, I_3) : 3$
I_2	$(I_1 : 2)$	$(I_1 : 2)$	$(I_1, I_2 : 2)$
I_1	$(I_5 : 3)$	$(I_5 : 3)$	$(I_5, I_1 : 3)$

Test Your Progress

1. What are the limitations of Apriorialgorithm.
2. Explain the phases of FP-Growth algorithm.
3. What is FP-tree?

3.5   Mining Multilevel Association Rules

Association rules generated from mining data at different levels of abstraction are known as multilevel association rules. This rule is generated on the basis of concept hierarchy with support and confidence measures. In general,Apriori algorithm and its variation is used for traversing the concept hierarchies and generating the frequent itemsetsby employing a top-down strategy. That means after determining the frequent itemsets at level i, frequent itemsets are generated for level i+1 and so on until no more frequent itemsets can be found.

Disadvantage of mining multilevel association rules is that it leads to generation of many redundant rules across multiple levels of abstraction due to the ancestor relationship between items.

Some of the variations of mining multilevel association rules are:

1. **Using uniform minimum support for all levels**

    In this method same minimum support is set to all levels of abstraction. This variation is easy to implement but it has some problems, such as first, items at the lower levels of abstraction may not occur often as those at higher levels of abstraction. Second, if minimum support threshold is set too high then it may skip some meaningful associations occurring at low abstraction levels. Third, if the minimum support threshold is set to as too low then it may generate many uninteresting associations occurring at high abstraction levels.

2. **Using reduced minimum support at lower levels**

    In this method, minimum support is set to different at all levels.

3. **Using item or group-based minimum support**

    In this method users and experts manually set the minimum support threshold at each level for abstraction. This setting is done on the basis of the importance of the itemsets.

3.6 Mining Multidimensional Association Rules

Association rules consisting of more than one dimension are called multidimensional association rule. These rules are classified into two types, such as inter-dimensional and hybrid dimensional. Inter-dimensional association rules do not involve repetition of some predicates on the other hand hybrid-dimensional association rules consist multiple occurrences of some predicates.

There are three basic approaches for mining multidimensional association rule to continuous attributes (quantitative). These are:

1. **Static discretization**

    In this approach, quantitative attributes are discretized in static and predetermined manner by using predefined concept hierarchies. Here, discretization occurs before mining and numeric value of attribute is replaced by ranges, such as "0.....10k". Then discretized with its range is treated as categorical attribute, where each interval is considered as category.

2. **Dynamic discretization**

    This approach, uses distribution of data to be discretized the quantitative attributes into bins. In this method, numeric attributes are dynamically discretized during the mining process.

3. **Distance-based**

    In this method quantitative attributes are discretized so as to capture the semantic meaning of interval data while allowing approximation in data values. To mine such rules, two steps are as follow:

    (a) Apply clustering algorithm to find the intervals, adapting to the amount of available memory.

    (b) Obtain distance-based association rules by searching for groups of clusters that occur frequently together.

Test Your Progress

1. What is the difference between multidimensional and multilevel association rules?

2. Explain the methods of multidimensional association rule.

3.7   Summary

Finally it has been concluded that association rule mining discovers relationships between the attributes in a database useful in marketing, decision analysis, business management and so on. Apriori and FP-growth algorithm are most popular algorithms to association rule mining. This Chapter also discussed multi-level and multi-dimensional association rules.

3.8   Key Terms

*   **Apriori algorithm:** An algorithm for frequent item set mining and association rule learning over transactional databases.

*   **FP-Growth algorithm:** An efficient and scalable method for mining the complete set of frequent patterns by pattern fragment growth, using an extended prefix-tree structure for storing compressed and crucial information about frequent patterns named Frequent-Pattern tree (FP-tree).

*   **Market basket analysis:** A concept in data mining involving the analysis of items frequently purchased together.

*   **Support:** The percentage of total transactions that satisfy antecedent and consequent of rule.

3.9   Exercise

1. Define association rule mining with example. Also relate it with market basket analysis.

2. How mining is performed on different kinds of association rules?

3. List shortcomings of the Apriori algorithm.

4. Discuss the various criteria for the classification of frequent pattern mining.

5. Define multi-dimensional association rule.

6. What is the need of FP-Growth algorithm?

University Questions

1. What is Concept/Class Description? **[UPTU 2008-09, 2009-10]**
    Refer section 2.1

2. What are the mining association rules in large database?
    OR
    What is Association Rule Mining? **[UPTU 2009-10, 2010-11,2012-13]**
    Refer section 3.1 and 3.2

3. Explain the Apriori Algorithm used for mining frequent item set for Boolean Association Rules. **[UPTU 2007-08, 2008-09, 2010-11, 2011-12,2012-13]**
    Refer section 3.4.1

4. What are multidimensional Association rules for mining from relational database and data warehousing? **[UPTU 2010-11]**
    Refer section 3.6

5. Explain the market basket analysis. Describe the basic concepts of association rule mining. **[UPTU 2011-12]**
    Refer section 3.2 and 3.1, 3.3

6. Discuss why analytical characterization and attribute relevance analysis are needed and how these can be performed? **[UPTU 2010-11, 2012-13]**
    Refer section 2.3

7. Explain mining multilevel association rules from transactional database.
    [UPTU 2012-13]
    Refer section 3.5

8. Describe statistical measures in large database. **[UPTU 2012-13]**
    Refer section 2.5

Unit-3

Classification and Predictions:What is Classification & Prediction, Issues regarding Classification and prediction, Decision tree, Bayesian Classification, Classification by Back propagation, Multilayerfeed-forward Neural Network, Back propagation Algorithm, Classification methods Knearestneighbor classifiers, Genetic Algorithm.

Cluster Analysis:

Data types in cluster analysis, Categories of clustering methods, Partitioning methods.Hierarchical Clustering- CURE and Chameleon.Density Based Methods-DBSCAN, OPTICS.Grid Based Methods- STING, CLIQUE.Model Based Method – Statistical Approach, Neural Network approach, Outlier Analysis

Chapter 4
Classification and Predictions

4.1 Introduction

Data analysis is one of the important parts of any application. Classification and prediction are two forms of data analysis to describe model classes and predict future trend respectively.

In the other words, data classification is a supervised learning refers to partitioning data into predefined disjoint groups or classes. Classification task is a two-step process:

Step 1: Model Construction (Classifier)

In this task build a model from the training set to predict the class of new items; given that items belong to one of the classes and given past instances of items along with the classes to which they belong. This model is represented as classification rules, decision tree or mathematical formulae.

Step2: Model Usage

This step is useful to check the accuracy of model by comparison of known class of data with the result given by model and classify unknown data. Accuracy of the classifier on a test set is defined as the percentage of test set tuples which are correctly classified by the classifier. If the associated class label of each test tuple matches with the learned classifier's class prediction of that tuple, the accuracy of the classifier is considered acceptable. This means that now the classifier can be easily used to classify future data for which the class label is not known.

Prediction is a continuous-valued function aims to predict unknown and missing values. This is also a two step process as to classification. In this process the model built during prediction is known as predictor, and the accuracy in prediction is estimated by computing the difference between the actual and predicted value of the predicted attribute for each of the test tuples. Regression analysis is a statistical methodology which is used in numeric prediction.

Tasks like a medical researcher wants to analyze brain tumour data in order to predict treatment a patient should receive, A bank officer analyze their data in order to learn loan applicants are "safe" or "risky" for the bank and so on are the examples of classification because classifier categorized data into class labels such as "treatment A" or "treatment B" and "safe" or "risky" applicant. Whereas when a market analyst wants to predict how much a customer will spend during sale at his company is called prediction.

Test Your Progress

1. What do you mean by classification and prediction?

2. Explain the two-step process of classification.

4.2   Issues Regarding Classification and Predictions

Classification and predictions methods suffer from various problems and issues which are categorized into two sub-fields, such as during pre-processing and another is to evaluating classification method.

1. **Issues of pre-processing of data for classification and prediction**

   a. **Data Cleaning:**This pre-processing step is helpful to reduce learning process by removing noisy data and by handle missing data from the dataset. Various techniques for removing noisy data and missing data are discussed in data mining.

   b. **Relevance Analysis:** It is a very important step to improve the classification efficiency and scalability. In this step irrelevant and redundant attributes should be removed from the learning process by using correlation analysis and attribute subset selection method. Correlation analysis method helps to identify whether two attributes are relevant or not, on the other hand attribute subset selection method is used to calculate the reduced set of attributes on the basis of probability distribution function.

   c. **Data Transformation and Reduction:** This step aims to generalize or normalize the data on the basis of concept hierarchy and neural network, respectively. Whereas data can also be reduced using various methods, such as wavelet transform, principal component analysis and so on.

2.   Issues to evaluating classification methods

a.   **Accuracy:** Classifier and predictor must be accurate in terms of ability of model to correctly identify class label of new or unseen data.

b.   **Speed:** It is on the basis of time to construct and use the model.

c.   **Robustness:** Ability to predict model with noisy and missing data.

d.   **Scalability:** Ability to construct the model with large amount of database.

e.   **Interpretability:** It is the level of understanding and insight that is provided by the model.

Test Your Progress

1.   Explain the limitations of classification and prediction.

2.   Why is correlation analysis method used?

4.3   Decision Tree Classifier

Decision tree classifier is a graphical representation of the classification rules. It is a flow chart-like tree structure which relates conditions and actions sequentially. Non-leaf node in the decision tree is labelled within an attribute which denotes a test on it. Every branch of decision tree indicates the final outcome of the test and every leaf node constitutes the label of the class. The node at the topmost level in the tree is termed as the **root node.** The learning of decision trees from class labelled training tuples is termed as **decision tree induction.**

An example is depicted in Figure 4.1. In this Figure attribute age is chosen as a partitioning attribute and four child nodes, one for each partitioning predicate 0-30, 30-50, 50-60 and over 60. For all these child nodes, the attribute income is chosen to further partition the training instances belonging to each child node. Depending on the value of the income, a class is associated with the customer. For example, if the age of customer is between 50-60 and his income is greater than 75,000 then the class associated with him is excellent.

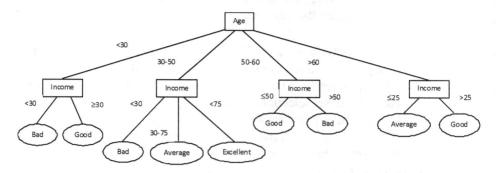

Figure 4.1: Decision tree

Test Your Progress

1. Explain the basic process of decision tree classifier.
2. What is decision tree induction?

4.3.1 Decision Tree Algorithms

1. **ID3 (Iterative Dichotomiser)**

   This algorithm was developed by J.Ross Quinlan in late 1970s which provided a broad approach for learning decision trees from training tuples. It essentially looks at complete stack of data and then determines which sets are more important than others, hence it attempts to minimize the expected number of comparisons.

2. **C4.5**

   This algorithm is a successor of ID3 which was developed by Quinlan. It became a benchmark to which newer supervised learning algorithms are often compared.

3. **CART (Classification and Regression Trees)**

   This algorithm was developed by a group of statisticians named L. Breiman J. Friedman, R.Olshen and C. Stone in 1984. It describes the generation of binary decision trees.

   All these algorithms follow a greedy approach. It means that the decision trees constructed by these algorithms are a top-down recursive divide-and-conquer approach. In such approach, the training set is recursively partitioned into smaller subset as the tree is being built. The algorithm searches attributes of the training set and extracts the attribute that best partitions the given instances. This attribute is called the partitioning (or splitting) attribute. If the partitioning attribute A, perfectly classifies the training set, the algorithm stops, otherwise it recursively selects the partitioning attribute and partitioning predicate to create further child nodes. The basic difference between these algorithms lies in the selection of attributes for construction of trees and the mechanisms used for pruning.

Test Your Progress

1. What are the various types of decision tree algorithms?
2. Who developed CART algorithm?

4.3.2 Advantages and Limitations of Decision Tree

Decision tree has various **advantages** such as, first, rules generated by decision trees can easily be translated into different formats like English, SQL (Structured Query Language) etc. Second, it provides an efficient choice in rule-oriented domains. There are many domains that have underlying rulessuch as, industrial processes, genetics etc., but all these domains tend to be more complex and contain noisy data. Noisy data, also cause misclassification. The decision tree method has an advantage over these domains, as this method takes care of missing values by working on them closely or by using surrogates to minimize their effect. Third, decision tree offers reduced complexity of calculations at the time of classifying rules. The algorithms which are used to generate decision trees generally yield trees with low branching factors and provide simple tests such as numerical computations, conjunction functions, etc., at every node of a tree. Fourth, it is very simple and straightforward for handling the continuous and categorical variables. Categorical variables come with their own splitting criteria which offer one branch for every category, thus making the splitting process is quite easy. Similarly, continuous variables are equally easy to split by selecting a number somewhere within their range of values.

Apart from various advantages there are mainly two **limitations** such as first, most of the algorithms require that the target attribute will have only discrete values, second, the process of decision tree induction is quite complex and requires huge computation costs which proves to be expensive. Every splitting field is required to be in sorted order before the best split is found. As several candidate sub-trees are required to build and compare in pruning algorithms, it therefore increases unnecessary costs.

Test Your Progress

1.   Explain the advantages and disadvantages of decision tree.

4.4   Bayesian Classification

Bayesian classification is a supervised learning as well as statistical method for classification, proposed by Thomas Bayes. It can predict class membership probabilities like a particular tuple belongs to a tuple. It is based on Bayes theorem described in section 6.4.1. Different Bayes classifiers have been developed:

i.   Joint density Bayes classifier

ii.   Naive Bayes classifier

iii.   Gaussian Bayes classifier

iv.   Other joint Bayes classifier possible

Bayesian classifiers can be successfully implemented on large databases with speed and with high accuracy.

4.4.1 Bayes Theorem

Bayes theorem states the relationship between conditional probabilities when some of the events are dependent on others. Such classification makes use of statistical classifiers which predicts the class membership probabilities that is, the probability that a given tuple belongs to a specific class. For classification problems, one needs to determine P(A/B), where A is referred to some hypothesis, and B is a data tuple belonging to a specific class C. In Bayesian term A is considered as evidence.

The representation of Bayes theorem is:

$$\mathbf{P\,(A/B)} = P(B/A)P(A) \div P(B)$$

Where, P (A/B): Probability of A conditioned on B

P (B/A): Probability of B conditioned on A

P (A): Probability of A

P (B): Probability of B.

For example, suppose our set of data tuple have age and income information, and B is a 30 year's old customer with its income of 40,000 INR and A be the hypothesis that customer will buy a laptop. Then P (A/B) will be the probability that B will buy a laptop, given age and income of the customer, while P (B/A) will be the probability that a customer is 30 years old and earn 40,000INR, given that they will buy a laptop. On the other hand, P (A) will be the probability that any given customer will buy a printer, regardless of his/her age or income. Similarly P (B) will be the probability that a person from our set of customers in 30 years old having income of 40,000 INR, irrespective of A.

4.4.2 Naive Bayesian Classification

It is a simple probabilistic classifier based on Bayesian statistics (Bayes theorem) and with strong independent assumptions (Naive), means effect of an attribute value on a given class is independent of the values of the other attributes. In other words, presence or absence of a specific feature of a class is not related to the presence or absence of any other feature in a given class. For example, a fruit may be considered to be a lemon if it is round, yellow, sour and about 2 inch in diameter. Although these features are related and dependent on each other or upon the existence of other features, but according to Naive Bayesian classifier all these features will be considered independent, and will contribute independently to the probability that this fruit is a lemon.

Simple Bayesian classifier is trained by using supervised learning. In various applications, it uses maximum likelihood parameter estimation method for better result. Various applications of naive Bayesian classifications are text classification, spam filtering, hybrid recommender system, online application and so on.

Advantages of Naive Bayesian classifiers

● They are less prone to errors and thus help in simplifying various computations involved.

● They provide a theoretical justification for other classifiers which do not use Bayes theorem explicitly.

● In spite of having oversimplified assumptions, they work well with real world situations.

● They require only a small amount of training data for parameter estimation.

4.4.3 Bayesian Belief Network

Unlike naive classifier, Bayesian belief network allows class conditional independence to be defined between subsets of variables. The network represents the set of random variables and their dependencies using two components, such as Directed Acyclic Graph (DAG) and Conditional Probability Table (CPT). A DAG consists of a set of interconnected nodes, where each node represents a random variable which can be any observable quantity, latent variable, unknown parameter or hypothesis, and the connecting edges represent the probabilistic dependence. For example, if there is an edge drawn from node A to node B, then it implies that A is a parent of B, and B is a child of A. However, a variable is considered to be conditionally independent if it is not connected to any other variable through an edge.

A DAG representing the casual knowledge between the cause and the result of sprinkle and rain is shown in Figure 4.2 which helps in computing the probabilities of the occurrence of sprinkle or rain with respect to their implied cause and result. It is simple belief network for four Boolean variables namely, cloudy, sprinkle, rain and wet grass. Here chances of sprinkle and rain depend on its parent that is cloudy. The edges show that these variables are conditionally dependent on each other.

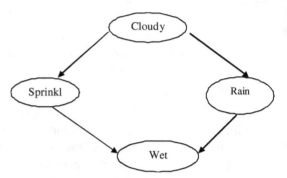

Figure 4.2: Direct Acyclic Graph

On the other hand, a belief network has one CPT for each variable. The CPT for a variable B specifies the conditional distribution P (B%Parents (B)), where Parents (B) are the parents of B. For example, CPT for variable Wet Grass (WG) is shown in Table 4.1. The conditional probability for each known value of WG is given for each possible combination of values of its parents.

It can be observed that:

$P(wet\ grass = yes|sprinkle = yes, rain = yes) = 0.99$

$P(wet\ grass = no|sprinkle = yes, rain = no) = 0.1$

Table 4.1 :CPT for the Variable Wet Grass (WG)

	S,R	S,~R	~S,R	~S,~R
WG	0.99	0.9	0.9	0.0
~WG	0.01	0.1	0.1	1.0

4.4.4 Bayes Error Rate

Bayes error rate is the minimum possible error rate for the given class, which is calculated in statistical classification. Basically two approaches of Bayes error rate has been discussed first, obtain analytical bounds which are totally dependent on distribution measures and second, dependent on class densities.

Bayes error rate is useful in machine learning and pattern classification. In this, data set has been divided into two or more classes. Each class or label must contain at least one element called **instance**.

For a single class, Bayes error rate is the probability of the classifier to incorrectly classify an instance, on the other hand multiclass bayes error rate calculated as:

$$P = \sum_{Ci \neq Cmax} \int_{x \in Hi} P(x|Ci)p(Ci)dx,$$

Where x is an instance of class C_i and H_i is the region that a classifier function h classified.

Test Your Progress

1. What is Bayesian classifier?
2. How to calculate Bayes error?
3. Explain Directed Acyclic Graph.
4. Define the advantages of Naive Bayesian classifier.
5. What is the importance of Bayes' theorem?

4.5 Neural Network for Classification and Prediction

Neural network is an important field to develop real-time applications. Origin of Neural network was to develop and test computational analogues of neurons. Neural networks learn by updating and adjusting the weights so that the correct class label of the input tuples can be predicted. Neural network algorithms usually run in parallel, which helps in speeding up the computation process and hence task become more efficient.

Various factors that make neural networks useful for classification and prediction in data mining are:

1. They provide high tolerance of noisy data.
2. They are able to classify those patterns on which they have not been trained.
3. They can be used in situations where the user has less knowledge of the relationships between attributes and classes.
4. Unlike most decision trees algorithms, they can be easily used for continuous-valued inputs and outputs.
5. They can be used for any kind of real-world data.
6. They employ parallelism to speed up the computation process.

Test Your Progress

1. What is the need of neural network in prediction?
2. Why is neural network algorithm run in parallel?

4.5.1 Multilayer Feed Forward Network

Multilayer network consists of input layer, one or more hidden layers and an output layer. Each layer is built up from several units. Units in the input layer are termed as **input units**, whereas the units in the hidden layers and output layers are referred to as **neurons**. Input layer consists of the attributes measured for each training tuple. These attributes serve as the inputs to the network. These inputs after passing through the input layer are weighted and then passed simultaneously to the hidden layer. As there can be more than one hidden layer, so output of one hidden layer would become the input of another hidden layer. Finally, the outputs of the last hidden layer are fed as inputs to the units of the output layer, which yields the network's prediction for given tuples. This network is also called feed-forward network in the sense that weights are always propagated only in the forward direction from input to hidden and from hidden to output layers. Figure 4.3 shows a multilayer feed-forward network.

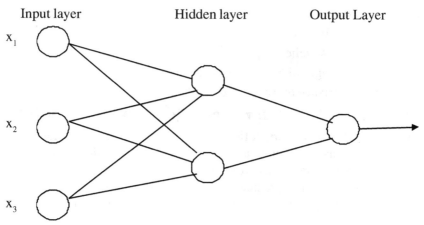

Figure 4.3: Multilayer Feed-forward Neural Network

4.5.2 Back Propagation Classifiers

Back propagation is a powerful and flexible neural network algorithm which performs learning on multilayer feed-forward neural network. Backpropagation algorithm learns by recursively processing a data set of training tuples and then comparing the prediction of the network for every tuple with the original target value. For classification problems, target value may be known as class label of the training tuple, and for prediction problems, it may be continuous value. For each training tuple, the weights are then modified such that the mean squared error between the network prediction and original target value is minimized. The modification in the weights is done in the backward direction, that is, from output layer through each hidden layer down to the first hidden layer. Hence, it is named as **backpropagation**.

Backpropagation summarizes into four major phases, which are described as:

Phase1: Weights initialization

In the first phase of backpropagation, firstly set the weights ranging from -1.0 to1.0 or –0.5 to0.5 in the multilayer feed-forward network. Bias is associated with each network unit to initialized small random number.

Phase 2: Propagate the input forward

In the second phase, inputs are fed into the input layers in the multilayer feed-forward network. Input of each k unit is passed unchanged so that output of unit k is equal to the input of unit k. Then net input and output of every unit in hidden and output layers are calculated as:

$$I_k = \Sigma_m W_{mk} O_m + \theta_k$$

And $O_k = 1/1 + e_k^{-1}$

Phase 3: Backpropagate the error

This phase is helpful to minimize error in between the hidden and output layers. In this step, error is propagate backward by updating the weights and biases. Error for unit k in the output layer calculated as:

$$Err_k = O_k (1 - O_k) (D_k - O_k)$$

Where O_k is the actual output for unit k and D_k is the targeted output value.

Now calculate the error of hidden layer unit k as:

$$Err_k = O_k (1 - O_k) (D_k - O_k) \Sigma_p Err_p W_{kp}$$

Where W_{kp} is the weight of the connection from unit k to unit p in the next higher layer, Err_p isthe error of unit p.

The weights are then updated to reflect the propagated errors as:

$$\Delta W_{mk} = (R) Err_k O_m$$
$$W_{mk} = W_{mk} + \Delta W_{mk}$$

Where $\ddot{A}W_{mk}$ is the change in weight W_{mk} and R is the learning rate, a constant having a value between 0.0 to 1.0.

Biases are also updated in the same way as weights are updated as:

$$\Delta\theta_k = (R) Err_k$$
$$\theta_k = \theta_k + \Delta\theta_k$$

Where $\Delta\theta_k$ is the change in the bias θ_k.

Since, the weights and biases are updated after every iteration; this strategy is known as **case updating.** On several instances, the weights and bias increments are accumulated in variables. This helps in updating the weights and biases after all the set of tuples in the training set have been used. Such strategy has been termed as **epoch updating** and each iteration through the training set is known as **epoch.**

Phase 4: Terminating condition

It is the last phase of backpropagation algorithm, it should be stopped within three conditions first, all the weights in the earlier iteration are less than the specified threshold, second, percentage of misclassified tuples in the last epoch is below some threshold, third, some pre-specified number of epoch have expired.

Test Your Progress

1. Explain the multilayer feed forward network.
2. What do you mean by forward network?

4.6   K-Nearest neighbour Algorithm

K-nearest neighbour classifier is one of the examples of lazy learner which is used in the area of pattern recognition. Lazy learner is a classification method in which the construction of a model is delayed until it is given a test tuple. Lazy learner simply stores the training tuple and waits until it is given a test tuple. Once the learner sees the test tuple, then it only performs generalization to classify the tuples on the basis of similarities of the stored training tuples. The k-nearest neighbour classifier learns by comparing a given test tuple with the training tuples that are similar to it. The similarity and closeness between two tuples is determined by Euclidean distance. Suppose we have two tuples X_1 and X_2 where $X_1 = (X_{11}, X_{12}, \ldots\ldots\ldots\ldots, X_{1n})$ and $X_2 = (X_{21}, X_{22}, \ldots\ldots\ldots\ldots X_{2n})$ represent that both the tuples are described by n attributes. Then, the distance between two tuples can be calculated as:

$$\text{Dist}(X_1, X_2) = \left[\sum_{i=1}^{n} (X_{1i}, X_{2i})^2 \right]^{1/2}$$

The k-nearest neighbour classifier basically stores all of the training tuple in an n-dimensional pattern space, where each tuple represents a point in this space. Now for a given unknown tuple, the k-nearest neighbour classifier searches the pattern space for the k training tuples that are closest or similar to the unknown tuple. K-nearest neighbour can be used for both classification and prediction. For classification, the unknown tuple is assigned among the most common class among its k-nearest neighbours while in prediction, the classifier returns the average value of the real-valued labels associated with the k-nearest neighbours.

However, if the attributes are of categorical type, then the distance is computed by comparing the corresponding value of the attribute in tuple X_1 with that in tuple X_2. If both tuples are identical, then the difference between the two is taken as 0 otherwise 1.

In Figure 4.4, let the new item be denoted by I, and A and B be the two classes to which I should be assigned. Now 'I' would be assigned to the class B because the six B's within the circle outnumbers the two A's. The k-nearest neighbours are considered as good predictors, robust to outliers and with the capability of handling the missing values. In general, if the value of a given attribute is missing in tuple X_1, and/or X_2 then one needs to consider the maximum possible difference. That is, if attribute is missing from both the tuples X_1, X_2 then difference value is taken as 1. If the attribute is categorical and its one value is missing and other value, v' is present, then the difference value is taken to be 1 only. On the other hand, if attribute is numerical and its one value is missing and other value v' is present then the difference which needs to be taken is either |1-v'| or |v'|, whichever is greater.

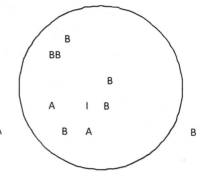

Figure 4.4: K-nearest Neighbor

Test Your Progress

1. Define k-nearest neighbour algorithm.

4.7 Genetic Algorithm

The term 'genetic algorithm' was first used in a book titled the 'origin of species', published by Charles Drawin in 1859. This book described how humans could be created and improved through the process of sexual reproduction. Genetic algorithms refer to the simulated evolutionary systems that create a version of biological evolution of computers. These algorithms are applied on the small computer programs that like living organisms can undergo natural evolution and are subject to medications and sexual reproduction. Over time, the performance of these small programs is improved, thereby achieving a high degree of competence. In simple words, this algorithm dictates how population of organisms should be formed, evaluated and modified. Here, organism represents the computer program being optimized and population refers to the collection of organisms undergoing simulated evolution. For example, there can be genetic algorithms which could determine how to select organisms for sexual reproduction while another could determine which organisms need not be removed for the population. Thus, one can say that this concept is based on the natural evolutionary process of search and optimization which helps in solving some real world problems. The real world problems that can be solved by genetic algorithms involve optimization of several data mining techniques, such as neural network and k-nearest neighbour.

In order to solve such real-world problems, one needs to determine how to convert the proposed solution to a complex real-world problem into simulated genetic material on a computer. For example, a company is doing a promotional mailing and wants to include free promotional coupons in the mailer. Now the question arises that what optimal number of promotional coupons should be put into a coupon mailer in order to gain maximum profit? At first, this problem seems easy to be solved. That is, to maximize the profits of consumers as well as company, mail out as many tickets as possible. However, there exist some complicated factors which would derive a company to make large profits. For instance, if there would be too many coupons in the mail, then customer will be overloaded and will not choose to use any of the coupons. Moreover, the higher the number of coupons, the more will be weight of the mailer. This would result in higher mailing costs and so will decrease the profit.

This problem can be easily solved by encoding it into a simple genetic algorithm where each simulated organism has a single gene representing the organism's best guess at the correct number of coupons. These computer programs will simply reflect the number of coupons that one should put into a mailer.

The genetic algorithm can proceed by randomly creating a population of these single-gene organisms. Then, it modifies the genes, deletes the worst performers and makes copies of the best performers through simulated evolution. Thus, it helps in determining the optimal number of coupons that would be needed. Figure 4.5 shows a population of coupon organisms, representing the number of organisms that need to be deleted and the number of organisms that need to be kept for further processing. As can be seen that in the first generation, the two simulated organism (one with 2 coupons and other with 2500 coupons) are deleted due to the low profitability of the mailers they proposed. The other two organisms (one with 15 coupons and other with 25 coupons) reproduced the similar copies of themselves into second generation which shows the optimal number of coupons that need to be put into the mailer. Although this is the simplest problem that can be solved by genetic algorithms, there can be several more complicated problems that can be efficiently solved by genetic algorithms. Moreover, the implementation of genetic algorithm in mining larger data sets has recently become popular due to the availability of high-speed computers.

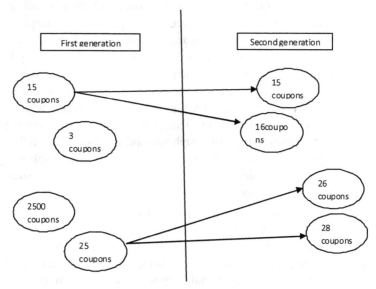

Figure 4.5: Populations of Coupons Organisms

There are various applications of genetic algorithm, these are:

1.   In financial data analysis: state street global advisors, advanced investment technologies, fidelity funds, PanAgora Asset Management.
2.   In engineering design: general electric, Boeing.
3.   Operations and supply chain management: general motors, Volvo, cemex.
4.   Machine learning.
5.   Combinatorial optimization: travelling salesman problem, factory scheduling.
6.   Function optimizer: difficult, discontinuous, noisy function, etc.

Test Your Progress

1.   What is genetic algorithm?
2.   Why is genetic algorithm useful in data mining?
3.   Explain the various applications of genetic algorithm.

4.8   Summary

This chapter summarizes classification and prediction into two form of data analysis that is identifying the class label and predicts the future trends, respectively. Various classifiers have been discussed, such as decision tree, Bayesian and neural network- based classifiers for practical scenario.

4.9   Key Terms

- **Bayes's theorem:** A theorem which supports the importance in the mathematical manipulation of conditional probabilities.
- **Decision tree classifier:** A graphical representation of the classification rules.
- **Directed acyclic graph:** A directed graph with no directed cycles.
- **ID3:** Iterative Dichotomiser 3; an algorithm which generates a decision tree from a dataset.

4.10   Exercise

1. How classification works?
2. How classification is different from prediction?
3. Why is decision tree classifier so popular?
4. What is Naive Bayesian classifier?
5. Describe backpropagation algorithm for neural network-based classification of data.
6. What is genetic algorithm?
7. Describe various methods which evaluate the accuracy of classifier or predictor.
8. What is the need of decision tree?

Chapter 5
Cluster Analysis

5.1   Introduction

A cluster is a collection of objects which has similar properties. The process of grouping the records into classes or clusters together so that the degree of association is strong between the records of same group and weak between the records of different groups is known as clustering or cluster analysis or sometime called data segmentation. Classification and clustering are two different concepts; clustering is an unsupervised learning that means it does not have training stage and no prior classes are defined whereas classification is a supervised learning, it is the reverse of unsupervised learning.

Test Your Progress

1.   Differentiate classification and clustering method.
2.   What is clustering?
3.   What is unsupervised learning?

5.2   Applications of Clustering

- Bio-informatics
- Handwriting recognition
- Medicine
- Information retrieval
- Psychiatry and archaeology
- Business and marketing
- Object recognition in computer vision
- Outlier detection
- Optical character recognition
- Spam detection
- Pattern recognition
- Speech recognition
- World Wide Web (WWW)
- Social Science
- Image processing

5.3 Data Types in Cluster Analysis

There are various types of data which can occur during cluster analysis task. These are:

1. **Quantitative variable:** It is a continuous variable that has positive and negative values both. It is measured on a linear scale.

2. **Binary variable:** It contains only two values, such as 0 and 1. Value 0 denotes variable is absent whereas value 1 shows the presence of value.

3. **Categorical variable:** These variables are the generalization of binary variables as they can take on more than two states like fruit name, etc.

4. **Ratio-Scaled variable:** It is a continuous positive measurement on a non-linear scale, such as exponential scale. For example, growth of the population.

5. **Vector objects:** It contains a large number of symbolic entities.

6. **Variables of mixed types:** It is a mixture of above variables.

Test Your Progress

1. Explain the types of data associated with clustering.

2. Write an example of radio-scaled variable.

5.4 Stages in Clustering

Clustering is not a one-step process; it can be done by various stages, such as:

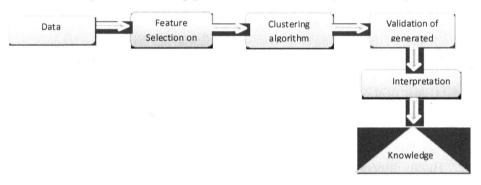

Figure 5.1: Stages of Clustering

Stage 1: Data

Firstly collect the relevant data from underlying data sources.

Stage 2: Feature Selection on data

Select features from the database on which clustering is to be performed.

Stage3: Clustering algorithm selection

In this step, user can select a clustering algorithm that generates good quality of clusters from the data set. Clustering algorithms are selected by two measures, such as proximity measure and clustering criteria. Proximity measures find how "similar" two data points are. Whereas in the clustering criterion step defines a cost function or some other types of rules to good clustering.

Stage4: Validation of generated clusters

It is an important step of clustering.The correctness of clustering algorithm results is verified using appropriate criteria and techniques.

Stage 5: Interpretation

Aim of this stage is to interpret the result. Sometimes experts want to integrate clustering results with other experimental results to make a decision.

Stage 6: Knowledge

It is a final stage to present a information for users.

Test Your Progress

1.   Define the phases of cluster analysis.
2.   Write the aim of Interpretation stage.

5.5   Requirements of Clustering in Data Mining

Some requirements of clustering in the field of data mining are described below:

1.   Scalability

Clustering algorithm must be scalable in terms of they can efficiently work on large databases.

2.   Immunity to noise data

Quality of data is a big issue in any application, but data may be inconsistent, noisy, outliers, not completed; in that case clustering algorithm should be immune towards such data.

3.   Ability to cluster different types of data

In real-time applications data should be of various types, such as numeric, multimedia, categorical, binary and so on. So clustering algorithm must be handling all data types.

4.   Highly dimensional

Data warehouse and database may be in multi-dimensional so clustering algorithm must capable to find clusters from those dimensions.

5.   Discovery of clusters with arbitrary shapes

Many clustering algorithms find spherical clusters which are similar in size and density by using Euclidean distance measures. However, such algorithms must be designed which can detect clusters of arbitrary shape and size.

6.   Minimum requirements for domain knowledge to determine input parameters

Many clustering algorithms may require input parameters from users so as to perform analysis. However, these parameters are difficult to determine for data sets containing high-dimensional objects and may cause quality control issues.

Therefore such algorithms must be designed which do not burden users in specifying input parameters.

7.   Insensitive to the order of input records and incremental clustering

Clustering algorithm must be insensible in terms of input and must follow incremental approach; therefore they must be able to incorporate newly inserted data into the clustering structures.

8.   Interpretable, comprehensive and usable

Algorithm must be easy to use, understandable by users.

Test Your Progress

1.   What are the requirements of cluster analysis in data mining?

2.   What is meant by scalability feature?

5.6   Challenges of Clustering

Clustering in high-dimensional spaces is a very hard problem due to the curse of dimensionality phenomenon and the presence of irrelevant features.

1.   Curse of dimensionality

The curse of dimensionality has to exist in any problem of data analysis that results from a large number of variables.For clustering purposes, the most relevant aspects for the curse of dimensionality are the impact of increasing dimensionality on point proximity and density.

In particular, distance-based clustering techniques depend critically on the measure of distance, and require that the objects within clusters are closer to each other than to objects in other clusters. Density-based clustering algorithms require that the point density within clusters must be significantly higher than the surrounding noise regions.

In moderate-to-high dimensional spaces almost all pairs of points are about as far away as average and the density of points inside a fixed-volume region is about as the average. Under such circumstances the data are "lost in space" and the effectiveness of clustering algorithms that depend critically on the measure of distance or density, degenerate rapidly with increasing dimensionality.

2.   Irrelevant Features - Subspace Clustering

Often, it may be possible that all dimensions are not relevant - the data are binded along such dimensions, to a given cluster. The presence of irrelevant features reduces any clustering tendency in the data. So, if we pruned all irrelevant features, then points in each cluster come closer to one another, making easier the discrimination of clusters using a distance or density based criterion. However, feature selection techniques are susceptible to a substantial loss of information because different types of inter-attribute correlations may occur in different subsets of dimensions in different localities of the data. Therefore, it is vital for any clustering algorithm to operate on the full-dimensional space.

5.7　Categorization of Clustering Methods

Clustering algorithms are broadly classified into four categories, such as:

- Partitioning
- Hierarchical
- Density-based
- Grid-based

5.7.1　Partitioning Clustering Methods

Partitioning clustering divides the data objects into k partitions or clusters such that partitions optimize a certain criterion function. Each cluster is shown by its centroid or by its medoid. Centroid is the centre of gravity of the cluster, for example K-means on the other hand medoid is the closest instance to the gravity centre. This method calculates sum of square but it should be minimum. One major drawback of partitioning algorithms is that there are a number of possible solutions by partitioning n patterns into k clusters is:

$$P(n,k) = \frac{1}{k!} \sum_{i=1}^{k} (-1)^{k-1} \left(\frac{k}{i}\right) (i)^n$$

Some representative examples of partitioning methods are: K-means, K-medoids, expectation maximization, Clustering Large Applications (CLARA), Clustering Large Applications based on Randomized Search (CLARANS).

K-means

K-means is the most popular partitioning clustering method in metric spaces. This algorithm can easily classify objects on the basis of attributes into k number of groups by minimizing the sum of squares of distances between object and corresponding group centroid. Here k is a user-defined groups which is called clusters. Process of k-means can easily understand by flow chart in Figure 5.2.

Step 1: Firstly decide the number of clusters by users.

Step 2: Classify the data into k number of clusters and canassign the training samples randomly or systematically as:

i.　Firstly use k training sample as k clusters with a single element.

ii.　After that assign remaining objects into those clusters with nearest centroid then recompute the centroid of the gaining cluster.

Step 3: In the third Step, compute the distance of each objects from its centroid of each clusters and place that objects with minimum distance centroid.

Step 4: Repeat Step 3 until no new object assignments remain into k number of clusters.

Despite its popularity k-means algorithm has some weaknesses, such as it is sensitive to outliers and noise, entrapments into local optima, it generates only spherical clusters, poor cluster descriptors, and predefined number of clusters without knowing database.

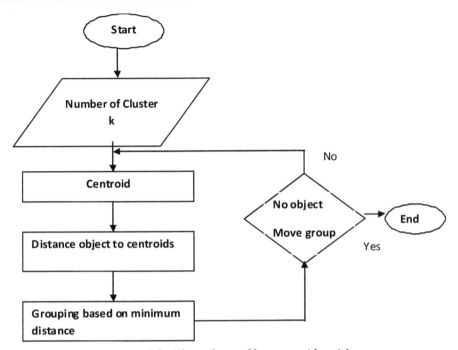

Figure 5.2: Flow chart of k-means Algorithm

Example 5.1:

Suppose there are four objects (types of medicines) and each object has two attributes or features as shown in Table 5.1.

Table 5.1: Set of Object

Object	Feature (X)	Feature (Y)
Object A	10	10
Object B	20	5
Object C	40	15
Object D	50	40

Solution: Let us solve the example 5.1 step-by-step using k-means algorithm.

1. **Initial value of centroids:** Suppose use the object A and object B as the first centroids. Let C_1 and C_2 denote the coordinates of the centroids, then $C_1 = (10,10)$ and $C_2 = (20,5)$ as shown in Figure 5.3.

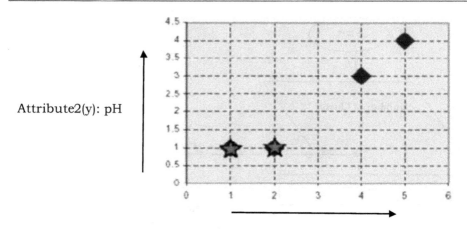

Attribute 1(x): weight index

Figure 5.3: K-mean Algorithm Iteration 0

2. **Objects-Centroids distance:** Calculate the distance between cluster centroid to each object and use Euclidean distance. Then distance matrix at iteration 0 is as follows:

$$D^0 = \begin{bmatrix} 0 & 11.18 & 30.41 & 50 \\ 11.18 & 0 & 20.61 & 46.3 \end{bmatrix} \begin{matrix} c_1 = (10,10) \ group-1 \\ c_2 = (20,5) \ group-2 \end{matrix}$$

$$\begin{matrix} A & B & C & D \\ \begin{bmatrix} 10 & 20 & 40 & 50 \\ 10 & 5 & 15 & 40 \end{bmatrix} & \begin{matrix} X \\ Y \end{matrix} \end{matrix}$$

Each column in the distance matrix symbolizes the object. The first row of the distance matrix corresponds to the distance of each object to the first centroid and the second row is the distance of each object to the second centroid. For example, distance from object $C = (40, 15)$ to the first centroid $C1 = (10,10)$ is $\sqrt{(40-10)^2 + (15-10)^2} = 30.41$ and its distance to the second centroid $C2 = (20,5)$ is $\sqrt{(40-20)^2 + (15-5)^2} = 20.61$, etc.

3. **Objects clustering:** Assign each object based on the minimum distance. Thus, object A is assigned to group 1, object B to group 2, object C to group 2 and object D to group 2. The element of Group matrix below is 1 if and only if the object is assigned to that group.

$$G^0 = \begin{bmatrix} 1 & 0 & 0 & 0 \\ 0 & 1 & 1 & 1 \end{bmatrix} \begin{matrix} group-1 \\ group-2 \end{matrix}$$
$$\quad A \quad B \quad C \quad D$$

4. **Iteration-l, determine centroids:** Knowing the member of each group, now compute the new centroid of each group based on these new memberships as shown in Figure 5.4. Group 1 only has one member thus the centroid remains in $C_1 = (10, 10)$. Group 2 now has three members, thus the centroid is the average coordinate among the three members:

$$c_2 = \left(\frac{20+40+50}{3}, \frac{5+15+40}{3} \right) = \left(\frac{110}{3}, \frac{60}{3} \right)$$

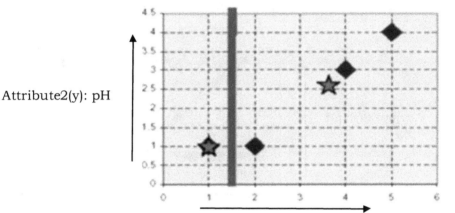

Attribute2(y): pH

Attribute 1(x): weight index

Figure 5.4: K-mean Algorithm Iteration 1

5. **Iteration-l, Objects-Centroids distances:** The next Step is to compute the distance of all objects to the new centroids. Similar to Step 2, distance matrix at iteration 1 is as follows:

$$D^1 = \begin{bmatrix} 0 & 11.18 & 30.41 & 5 \\ 19.43 & 21.93 & 6.01 & 20.04 \end{bmatrix} \begin{matrix} c_1 = (10,10) \ group-1 \\ c_2 = \left(\dfrac{110}{3}, \dfrac{60}{3} \right) group-2 \end{matrix}$$

$$\quad A \quad B \quad C \quad D$$

$$\begin{bmatrix} 10 & 20 & 40 & 50 \\ 10 & 5 & 15 & 40 \end{bmatrix} \begin{matrix} X \\ Y \end{matrix}$$

6. **Iteration-1, Objects clustering:** Similar to Step 3, we assign each object based on the minimum distance. Based on the new distance matrix, we move the object B to Group 1 while all the other objects remain. The Group matrix is shown below.

$$G^1 = \begin{bmatrix} 1 & 1 & 0 & 0 \\ 0 & 0 & 1 & 1 \end{bmatrix} \begin{matrix} gruop-1 \\ group-2 \end{matrix}$$
$$\quad\; A \;\; B \;\; C \;\; D$$

7. **Iteration 2, determine centroids:** Now repeat Step 4 to calculate the new centroids coordinate based on the clustering of previous iteration (see Figure 5.5). Group 1 and group 2 both have two members, thus the new centroids are:

$$C_1 = \left(\frac{10+20}{2}, \frac{10+5}{2} \right) = and\ C_2 = \left(\frac{40+50}{2}, \frac{15+40}{2} \right)$$

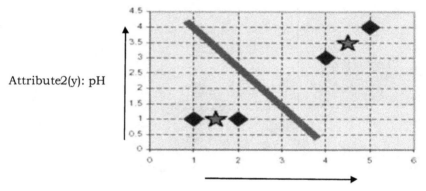

Attribute2(y): pH

Attribute 1(x): weight index

Figure 5.5: K-mean Algorithm Iteration 2

8. **Iteration-2, Objects-Centroids distances :** Repeat Step 2 again, then new distance matrix at iteration 2 is as follows:

$$D^2 = \begin{bmatrix} 5.59 & 5.59 & 26.1 & 47.76 \\ 39.13 & 33.63 & 13.46 & 13.46 \end{bmatrix} \begin{matrix} c_1 = (15,7.5)\ group-1 \\ c_2 = (45,27.5)\ group-2 \end{matrix}$$
$$\quad\;\; A \;\; B \;\; C \;\; D$$
$$\begin{bmatrix} 10 & 20 & 40 & 50 \\ 10 & 5 & 15 & 40 \end{bmatrix} \begin{matrix} X \\ Y \end{matrix}$$

9. **Iteration-2, Objects clustering:** Again, assign each object based on the minimum distance.

$$G^2 = \begin{bmatrix} 1 & 1 & 0 & 0 \\ 0 & 0 & 1 & 1 \end{bmatrix} \begin{matrix} group-1 \\ group-2 \end{matrix}$$

$$\quad\quad A \quad B \quad C \quad D$$

Obtain result that $G^2 = G^1$ means computation of the K-means clustering has reached its stability and no more iteration is needed and gets the final grouping as the results summarized in Table 5.2.

Table 5.2: Result of clustering

Object	Attribute 1 (X)	Attribute 2 (Y):	Group (result)
Object A	10	10	1
Object B	20	5	1
Object C	40	15	2
Object D	50	40	2

K-medoids

Unlike k-means, in the k-medoids or Partitioning AroundMedoids (PAM) method, a cluster is represented by its medoid, that is the most centrally located object (pattern) in the cluster. In this algorithm first randomly select an object as medoid for each of the k clusters after those non-selected objects merged with those clusters with its similarity bases.The k-medoids algorithm can handle noise and outliers easily as compare to k-means algorithm.

Clustering Large Applications (CLARA)

CLARA is an implementation of PAM, basically it a subset of PAM. This algorithm classifies subset of database after that applies PAM on samples, and then calculates clustering results.

Clustering Large Applications based on Randomized Search (CLARANS)

CLARANS is basically a combination of PAM and sampling techniques. This method representing as a searching graph where each node has a potential solution that is a set of k-medoids. CLARANS selects a node and compares it to a user-defined number of neighbors searching for a local minimum. If found lower square error then switch to the neighbor's node and the process starts again; otherwise starts with a new randomly selected node.

Advantages and Disadvantages of Partitioning Clustering

Advantages

● It is simple and scalable.
● Most appropriate for datasets with compact spherical clusters.

Disadvantages

● Poor in terms of cluster descriptors.

- Noise and outlier detection both are difficult.
- Define number of clusters prior without knowing about database.
- It should stuck into local minima.

5.7.2 Hierarchical Clustering Methods

Unlike partitioning methods that create a single partition, hierarchical algorithms produce a nested sequence (or dendrogram) of clusters with a single all inclusive cluster at the top and singleton clusters of individual points at the bottom. The hierarchy can be formed in top-down (divisive) or bottom-up (agglomerative) fashion and need not necessarily be extended to the extreme.

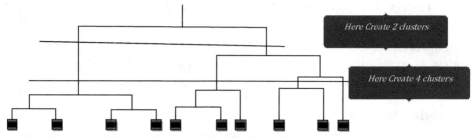

Figure 5.6: Hierarchical Clustering

The merging or splitting stops once the desired number of clusters has been formed. Typically, each iteration involves merging or splitting a pair of clusters based on a certain criterion, often measuring the proximity between clusters. Hierarchical techniques suffer from the fact that previously taken steps (merge or split), possibly erroneous, are irreversible. Some representative examples are: AGNES and DIANA, Clustering Using Representatives (CURE), CHAMELEON, Balanced Iterative Reducing and Clustering using Hierarchies (BIRCH).

Agnesand Diana

Agglomerative Nesting (AGNES) and Divisive Analysis (DIANA) are two earlier bottom-up and top-down hierarchical clustering methods, respectively. In both AGNES and DIANA, the similarity or dissimilarity between clusters is computed using the distance between the cluster representative points, for example centroids or closest points. Both methods are irreversible and use over-simplified static rules to split or merge clusters which may lead to low quality clustering. Finally, they do not scale well since the decision to merge or split needs to examine and evaluate many combinations of clusters.

Clustering Using Representatives (CURE)

It is a hierarchical clustering technique that adopts an agglomerative scheme. CURE algorithm is efficient in handling large databases and has got the ability to identify clusters of non-spherical shapes. In this algorithm, each cluster is represented by a centroid point; however the centroid point works well only with spherical-shaped clusters. However in real life situations clusters can be of arbitrary shapes.

For such situations, the centroid cannot represent the clusters. In such cases, CURE algorithm is used. In this algorithm each cluster is represented by a set of well-scattered points so as to properly represent the whole cluster. The set of representative points is reasonably smaller in number so as to reduce the computations effort and time. It can easily handle the outliers.

The algorithm begins by randomly choosing a constant number of points, C, from each cluster. These well-scattered points are then shrunk towards the cluster's centroid by applying a shrinking factor (?). Shrinking operation is performed to weaken the effect of outliers. When the value of? is 1, all points are shrunk to the centroid. These points represents the clusters better than a centroid, and also, can better represent the non-spherical clusters. CURE then uses a hierarchical clustering algorithm. It begins by treating every single object as a cluster where the object itself is the sole representative of the corresponding cluster. At any given stage of the algorithm, one has a set of subclusters associated with a set of representative points. The two subclusters with the closest pair of representative points are chosen to be merged. The distance between them is defined as the smaller pair-wise distance between their representative points. Once the clusters are merged, a new set of points is computed for the merged cluster. That is algorithm finds the farthest objects from the centroid of new cluster to have the first representative point. This is subsequently repeated to find other representative points by choosing a point in the subcluster which is farthest from the previously chosen representative points. These points are then shrunk towords the centroid by a factor ?.

Chameleon

CHAMELEON is more effective than CURE in discovering arbitrary-shaped clusters of varying density. CHAMELEON improves the clustering quality then CURE by using more elaborate merging criteria. This algorithm completed in two phases initially, a graph containing links between each point and its k-nearest neighbors is created after that apply graph-partitioning algorithm recursively to split the graph into small-unconnected sub-graphs. In the second phase, each sub-graph represents as a sub-cluster and an agglomerative hierarchical algorithm repeatedly combines the two most similar clusters. Clusters can be merged if and only if the resultant cluster has similar inter-connectivity.

Balanced Iterative Reducing and Clustering using Hierarchies (BIRCH)

This clustering method uses a novel hierarchical data structure, CF-tree, for compressing the data into many small sub-clusters and after that performs clustering on these sub-clusters not onto the raw data. Sub clusters store compact summaries of data, called Cluster-Features (CF) that are stored in the leafs. The non-leaf nodes store the sums of the CF of their children. CF-tree is built by single scan of the dataset, in this tree object is inserted in the closest leaf entry. Once the CF-tree is built, any partitioning or hierarchical algorithms can use it to perform clustering in main memory. BIRCH is faster and incremental technique, it can easily handles outliers too but it has two major limitations, such as data order sensitivity and it cannot support non-spherical clusters because the concept of diameter to control the boundary of a cluster.

Advantages and Disadvantages of Hierarchical Clustering

Advantages

- Granularity levels should be flexible.
- It overcomes the problem of point linkages.

Disadvantages

- Once splitting or merging decision has to be done, these algorithms are unable to make corrections.
- Uncertain termination criteria.
- Prohibitively expensive for high-dimensional and massive datasets.
- Lack of interpretability in case of cluster descriptors.
- Due to the curse of dimensionality performance will be degraded into high-dimensional spaces.

5.7.3 Density-Based Clustering Methods

In this method, the data are clustered on the basis of their density (number of objects or data points). In such methods, the given cluster is made to expand as long as the density in the neighbourhood exceeds some threshold. That is for each object within a given cluster, the neighbourhood of a given radius has to contain at least a minimum number of objects. Unlike other methods, these methods do not cluster objects on the basis of the distance between the objects and hence can discover clusters of arbitrary shapes. In addition, such methods can also be used to filter out noise. Some examples are Density-Based Spatial Clustering of Applications with Noise (DBSCAN), Ordering Points to Identify the Clustering Structure (OPTICS), Density-based Clustering (DENCLUE).

Density-Based Spatial Clustering of Applications with Noise (DBSCAN)

It is a density-based clustering algorithm which creates clusters with a minimum size and density. That is, this algorithm grows regions with sufficiently high density into clusters and discovers clusters of arbitrary shape in spatial database containing noise. Some of the terms associated with this method are as follows:

i. **ε (Eps or Epsilon) neighbourhood**: For each point in a cluster, there must be another point in the cluster whose distance from it is less than a threshold input value, ε. The ε-neighborhood of a point is then the set of points within a distance of ε.

ii. **MinPts:** It indicates the minimum number of objects in any cluster.

iii. **Core object:** An object is said to be a core object if the ε-neighborhood of an object contains at least MinPts of objects.

iv. **Directly density reachable:** Given a set of objects D, then an object p is said to be directly density reachable from object q if p is within the ε- neighborhood of q, and q is a core object.

v. **Density-reachable:** Given a set of objects D, then an object p is said to be density reachable from object q with respect to ε(Eps) and MinPts in a given set of objects (D), if there exists a chain of objects p_1......, p_n, where $p_1 = q$ and $p_n = p$, such that p_{i+1} is directly density reachable from p_i with respect to ε(Eps) and MinPts, for $1 \leq i \leq n$, ($P_i \varepsilon D$).

vi. **Density connected:** An object p is said to be density connected to object q with respect to ε (Eps) and Minpts in a set of objects D, if there exists an object o belongs to D such that both p and q are density reachable from o with respect to ε and Minpts.

vii. **Density-based cluster:** It is defined as a set of density connected an object that is maximal with respect to density-reachability.

viii. **Border point:** A directly density-reachable objects must be close to one of the core points, but it need not be a core point itself. In that case, the point is said to be border point.

ix. **Noise:** objects not assigned to any cluster are considered as noise.

In this algorithm first checks for the •-neighborhood of each point in the database. If the •-neighborhood of a point q contains more than MinPts, a new cluster is created in which q acts as the core object. After that algorithm iteratively collects directly density-reachable objects from these core objects, which may result in the merging of some density-reachable clusters. This process terminates when there is no new point to add to any cluster.

Ordering Points to Identify the Clustering Structure (OPTICS)

This algorithm is helpful to generate density-based clusters in dataset. Basically Ordering Points To Identify the Clustering Structure (OPTICS) is an extension of DBSCAN with adapt local densities. DBSCAN suffers a major weakness, such as problem of detecting meaningful clusters with varying density. To overcome this limitation of DBSCAN, OPTICS drawn the points of database in an linear order such that points which are spatially closest become neighbours in the ordering. It also stores some additional distance information, allowing the extraction of all density-based clustering for any lower value of the radius.

Density-based Clustering (DENCLUE)

This algorithm based on a set of density distribution functions. This method is built on some ideas, which are as follows:

i. The impact/influence of an object within its neighbourhood can be described using a mathematical function, known as an **influence function**. It is an arbitrary that can be determined by the distance between two objects in a neighbourhood.

ii. The overall density of the data space can be modelled analytically as the sum of the influence function applied to all objects.

iii. Clusters can then be determined mathematically by identifying density attractors. These attractors refer to the local maxima of the overall density function.

To compute the sum of influence functions a grid structure is used. DENCLUE finds the arbitrary shape of clusters and find the outlier efficiently but suffers from its sensitivity to the input parameters.

Advantages and Disadvantages of Density-based Clustering

Advantages

- Data types vary according to real-time applications; in that case these algorithms are generating arbitrary-shaped of clusters.
- Easy to handle noise and outliers.

Disadvantages

- These algorithms have weak cluster descriptors.
- These algorithms are not performing well for high-dimensional datasets because of the curse of dimensionality.

5.7.4 Grid-Based Clustering Methods

In these methods, there is quantization of objects space into a finite number of cells to form a grid-like structure. All the clustering operations can be performed on this grid like structure. The processing time of this approach is much faster as it is dependent only on the number of cells present in each dimension in the quantized object space and not on the number of data objects in the dataset. STING and WaveCluster are examples of grid-based clustering methods.

STING: (A STatisticalINformation Grid Approach to Spatial Data Mining)

It is a grid-base multi-resolution clustering technique. In this method, spatial area is divided into rectangular cells forming a hierarchical structure. There are usually several levels of cells which correspond to different levels of resolution. Each cell at the higher-level is partitioned to form a number of cells at the next lower-level. These cells store the statistical information of the higher-level cells could be easily computed from the parameters of the lower-level cells.

The statistical parameters include the following:

i. The attribute independent parameter, such as count.

ii. The attribute dependent parameters, such as mean, min, max, etc.

iii. The type of distribution that the attribute value in the cell follows, such as normal, uniform, exponential or none.

Parameters min, max, mean of the lower-level cells are calculated directly from the data. On the other hand, the value of distribution of lower-level cell may either be assigned by the user if the distribution type is known beforehand or could be obtained by the hypothesis test. The value of distribution type of higher-level is computed on the basis of the value of distribution type of its corresponding lower-level cells in conjunction with a threshold filtering process. The value is set to none if the distributions of the lower-level cells disagree with each other and fail the threshold test. The statistical information is very useful in answering queries and can be used in a top-down, grid-based method as follows:

- The layer which typically contains a small number of cells is determined from the hierarchical structure. Here query-answering process is started.
- For each cell in the current layer, confidence interval is computed which reflects the cell's relevance to the given query.
- The cells are then labelled as relevant or irrelevant on the basis of calculated value. The irrelevant cells are removed from further consideration and only the remaining relevant cells are examined for processing of the next lower level. This process is repeated until the bottom layer is reached.
- If the query specifications are met, then the regions of the relevant cells that specify the given query are returned; otherwise the data that fall into the relevant cells are retrieved and further processed until they meet the requirements of the given query.

Wave Cluster

It summarizes the data by imposing a multi-dimensional grid structure onto the data space and then applies a wavelet transformation to transform the original feature space to find dense regions in such transformed space. Each cell of a grid contains summarized information about the group of objects, which fits into main memory so that it can be used for performing multiresolution wavelet transformation and subsequent cluster analysis.

A wavelet transform is a single processing technique that decomposes a signal into several frequency sub-bands such technique can be applied to n-dimensional signals by applying one-dimensional wavelet transform n times. While applying a wavelet transform, data are transformed in such a manner that they do not affect the relative distance between objects at various levels of resolution. This allows the natural clusters in the data to become more distinguishable, and hence clusters could then be easily identified by searching for dense regions in the new domain.

Advantages and Disadvantages of Grid-based Clustering

Advantages

- These algorithms are depends on number of cells not depend upon the number of objects so that processing time is very fast.
- Cluster neighboring can be easily found.
- By using these algorithms grid-cells shapes are limited.

Disadvantages

Main disadvantage of Grid-based clustering is that the quality of clustering is dependent on the granularity of cells and that the number of cells increases exponentially with the dimensionality of data.

5.7.5 Model-based Method

In these methods, a model is hypothesized for each of the clusters and the model on which data can be best fitted is then discovered. A model-based method may also determine clusters with the help of density function which reflects the spatial distribution of the data points. It is one of the robust clustering techniques as it can automatically determine the number of clusters by taking noise into consideration. These methods include several algorithms, such as EM (Expectation Maximization,performs expectation-maximization analysis based on statistical modelling), COBWEB (which performs probability analysis), SOM (Self-Organizing Map, based on neural networks and performs clustering by mapping high dimensional data into Two-dimensional or Three dimensional feature map).

Expectation Maximization

The Expectation Maximization (EM) algorithm represents each cluster using a probability distribution instead of representing a cluster with a single point. EM is an example of fuzzy clustering where each object is assigned a certain degree of membership to each cluster. Similar to k-means and k-medoids, EM iteratively modifies the membership of each object until a likelihood based criterion function converges. EM is frequently entrapped into local optima.

Test Your Progress

1.   Classify the clustering techniques.

2.   Compare partitioning and hierarchical clustering methods.

3.   Explain the advantages and disadvantages of density-based method.

5.8   Clustering Techniques for High-Dimensional Dataset

Most clustering techniques till now are discussed for clustering low-dimensional data. However for high-dimensional data, there are some challenges which are faced by clustering techniques. They are:

i.   When the dimensionality of data grows, then it is seen that only small number of dimensions are relevant to certain clusters.

ii.   Data in the irrelevant dimensions may produce noise which in turn makes the discovery of real clusters.

iii.   With increase in dimensionality, data become increasingly sparse, by which the objects located at different dimensions can be considered as at equal distance. Thus, distance measure which is the most important element of cluster analysis become insignificant.

To overcome these problems, following techniques were introduced:

1.   Feature Transformation

This technique transforms the data onto a smaller space while preserving the original relative distance between objects. They summarize the data by creating linear combinations of the attributes and may even discover hidden structures in the data. However, such techniques do not actually remove any of the original attributes from the analysis. This makes them suitable only for those datasets where most of the dimensions are relevant to the clustering task. That is, this technique is not suitable when there are large numbers of irrelevant attributes. The irrelevant attributes may mask the real clusters, even after transformation. Examples of such techniques include Principal Component Analysis (PCA) and singular value decomposition.

2.   Feature subset selection

This technique is commonly used for reducing data by removing the irrelevant or redundant attributes. That is, it finds only that subset of attributes from a given set of attributes that are most relevant to the data mining task. This is most commonly performed using supervised learning in which the most relevant set of attributes is searched with respect to the given class labels. It can also be performed by unsupervised learning, which is based on property that entropy tends to be low for data that contain tight clusters.

3.   Subspace Clustering:

This technique is an extension to attribute subset selection. It is based on the observation that different subspaces may contain different, meaningful clusters and therefore, searches for groups of clusters within different subspaces of the same dataset.

Test Your Progress

1.   Explain the limitation of low dimensional clustering techniques.

2.   How to overcome low dimensional clustering techniques limitations?

5.9   Neural Network Approach in Clustering

Neural network approach is motivated by biological neural network which is in turn inspired from neuroscience. Neural networks are computing system, which imitate human brain through a network of highly interconnected processing elements. These processes give these networks learning capabilities and enable them to recognize and understand complex patterns. The key element of neural network is the presence of the information processing system. This system is composed of a large number of highly interconnected processing elements called **neurons** working together to solve specific problems. Neural network is just like human learn by example. That is, they are configured for a specific application such as pattern recognition or data classification through a learning process.

A perceptron is one of the earliest neural network models, in which neurons takes weighed sum of inputs and sends the output if sum is greater than any adjustable threshold value. The input in a perceptron is $x_1, x_2, \ldots \ldots \ldots x_n$ and connection weights are $w_1, w_2, \ldots \ldots w_n$. If the presence of some feature x_i tends to cause the perceptron to fire, the weight w_i will be positive and if the feature x_i inhibits the perceptron, the weight w_i will be negative.

Neural network take a different approach to solve a problem as compared to conventional computers. Conventional computer follows a set of instructions in order to solve a problem and requires specific steps to solve a problem. This restricts the problem-solving capability of conventional computers to problems whose solution are already known. Neural network's ability to learn by example makes it a very flexible and powerful concept. There is a no need to devise an algorithm in order to perform a specific task, that is, there is no need to understand the internal mechanisms of problem.

Traditional artificial intelligence and neural network are generally considered appropriate for solving different types of problems. These two approaches appear to be different, but currently the strengths of both the concepts are merged together to develop a system that includes the best features of both these approaches. The neural network has been applied successfully in the artificial intelligence field for speech recognition, image analysis, construct software agent, adaptive control, autonomous robot and so on.

Neural networks have several properties that make them popular for clustering. These are as follows:

i.   They employ parallel and distributed processing architectures.

ii. They have the capability of learning by adjusting their interconnection weights in such manner that the best fits the data. This enables them to normalize the patterns and act as feature extractors for different clusters.

iii. They are capable of processing numerical vectors and require object patterns to be represented by quantitative features only.

In clustering, neural network approach represents each cluster as an exemplar. An exemplar acts as a prototype of the cluster and does not necessarily have to correspond to a particular data example or object. On the basis of some distance measure, new objects are distributed to those clusters whose exemplar is most similar. Self-organizing feature maps are one of the most popular neural network methods for cluster analysis. Goal of SOMs is to represent all objects in a high-dimensional source space by points in a low-dimensional target space in such a manner that the distance and proximity relationships are preserved to a maximum extent.

Test Your Progress

1.   How neural network approach is useful in clustering?
2.   Write some applications of artificial intelligence.
3.   Discuss the properties of neural networks that make them popular for clustering.

5.10 Outlier Analysis

Data objects which are quite different or inconsistent in comparison with remaining set of data are known as **outliers**as shown in Figure 5.7.

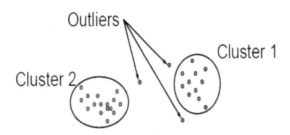

Figure 5.7: Clusters and Outliers

Such kind of data objects usually do not comply with the general behaviour of the data and can occur because of some measurement errors or may be present as a result of inherent data variability. For example, age of a person can be displayed as 55 by a program default setting of an unrecorded or unknown age. Most mining algorithms effortlessly try to reduce the effect of outliers or eliminates them completely. However this can lead to the huge loss of important hidden information because in some cases the outliers are of particular interest,such as in the case of fraud detection, where outliers may indicate fraudulent activities. The technique used to identifying and mining such outliers is termed as **outlier mining.** The outlier mining is widely used in different applications such as in the detection of fraudulent activities (misuse of credit cards, bank accounts, etc.), in observing spending trends of customers with extremely high or low incomes, in medical analysis to identify unusual responses from a patient to a particular treatment and so on.

Suppose a set of n objects is given which is having expected number of outliers as k. Then, outlier mining task is to find the top k objects that are considerably dissimilar or inconsistent with respect to the remaining data.

The outlier mining problem consists of two key phases:
1. Identifying the inconsistent data in a given dataset.
2. Finding an efficient method for extracting the defined outliers.

The problem of defining outliers is not much difficult for numerical data but for non-numeric and time-series data, the definition of outliers becomes complicated.

Generally using data visualization methods for detecting outliers is an obvious choice since human beings are quite efficient in detecting inconsistencies among data. There are various areas where data values appear to be outliers but could be perfectly valid values in reality. Such methods are also not a good alternative when datasets have many categorical attributes as humans are good at visualizing numeric data of only two or three dimensions. Therefore for efficient outlier detection some computer-based methods have been developed, such as statistical distribution-based, distance-based and density-based and deviation-based outlier detection.

Test Your Progress
1. What is outlier analysis?
2. Discuss the key phases of outlier miming problem.

5.11 Summary

This Chapter discuss about the various clustering algorithms with their advantages and disadvantages, where these algorithms are applicable, role of clustering in the field of data mining and neural network, and fraudulent behaviour analysis using outlier analysis.

5.12 Key Terms

- **Clustering:** The task of grouping a set of objects in such a way that objects in the same group, called a cluster, are more similar to each other than to those in other groups (clusters).

- **Curse of Dimensionality:** A process which refers to various phenomena that arise when analyzing and organizing data in high-dimensional spacesthat do not occur in low-dimensional settings such as the three-dimensional physical space of everyday experience.

- **DBSCAN:** A simple and effective density-based clustering algorithm that illustrates a number of important concepts supporting density-based clustering approach.

5.13 Exercise

1. Write algorithms for k-means and k-medoid.
2. Explain outlier analysis in detail.
3. Define grid-based clustering method.
4. Explain different types of data used in cluster analysis.
5. What is the need of clustering?
6. Explain the importance of neural network approach in clustering.
7. What are the requirements of clustering in data mining?
8. Define one of the clustering methods for high-dimensional database.

University Questions

1. What is Classification? Explain with example.   **[UPTU 2009-10, 2011-12]**
   Refer section 4.1
2. What are the Issues regarding classification and prediction?
   [UPTU 2008-09, 2009-10]
   Refer section 4.2
3. Describe the decision tree with example. How is classification done by decision tree Induction?   **[UPTU 2008-09, 2009-10, 2010-11]**
   Refer section 4.3.1
4. Describe Bayesian Classification.   **[UPTU 2011-12,2013-14].**
   What is Bayes Theorem?   **[UPTU 2008-09]**
   Refer section 4.4 and 4.4.1

5. Describe Multilayer Feed Forward Neural Networks?
    [UPTU 2009-10,2010-11]
    Refer section 4.5.1

6. What is Back Propagation?   **[UPTU 2008-09,2013-14]**
    Refer section 4.5.2

7. What is Cluster Analysis?   **[UPTU 2007-08, 2008-09, 2009-10]**
    Refer section 5.1

8. What are the types of data that occurs in Cluster Analysis?
    [UPTU 2008-09, 2011-12]
    Refer section 5.3

9. What is Hierarchical clustering? Explain the two types of Hierarchical methods
    clustering.   **[UPTU 2003-04, 2008-09]**
    Refer section 5.7.3

10. Describe the Density-Based Clustering Method DBSCAN. **[UPTU 2010-11]**
    Refer section 5.7.3

11. What is outlier Analysis? **[UPTU 2012-13]**Explain the outliner Detection.
    [UPTU 2009-10]
    Refer section 5.10

12. What is a decision tree?   **[UPTU 2013-14]**
    Explain the classification bydecision tree induction. Describe the tree pruning.
    [UPTU 2010-11]
    Refer section 4.3.1

13. Describe the neural network. How the neural networkuseful in classification?
    Explain.   **[UPTU 2009-2010, 2010-11]**
    Refer section 5.9

14. What are the different classification techniques? Discuss issues regarding
    classification and prediction.   **[UPTU 2009-10]**
    Refer section 4.1 and 4.2

15. What is clustering? How is this different than classification? Explain atleast
    one approach of clustering.   **[UPTU 2011-12]**
    Refer section 5.1

16. Define CLIQUE and STING.   **[UPTU 2012-13]**
    Refer section 5.7.4

17. Describe the role of genetic algorithm in data mining.
    [UPTU 2012-13, 2013-14]
    Refer section 4.7

18. Define Hierarchical and non-hierarchical clustering.   **[UPTU 2013-14]**
    Refer section 5.7

Unit-4

Data Warehousing: Overview, Definition, Delivery Process, Difference betweenDatabase System and Data Warehouse, Multi Dimensional Data Model, Data Cubes,Stars, Snow Flakes, Fact Constellations, Concept hierarchy, Process Architecture, 3 TierArchitecture, Data Marting.

Chapter 6
Introduction to Data Warehouse

6.1   Overview and Definition of data warehouse

Now-a-days data warehouse is an important part of companies. Databases offer basic data storage and retrieval solution business require a more sophisticated system. Many large companies have spent huge amount to develop enterprise wide data warehouse.For example, any travel company like abc.com requires some data from the past like in summer how many people like to travel Jaisalmer for vacation. They can use this information from the past to plan and decide their strategies in the current year. However, some additional information like at which season the most tourists come plays important role in deciding the strategies too. This type of information from the past gives an idea to the company and it helps in future actions to be taken.

A data warehouse is a collection of data marts representing historical data from different operations in the company. This data is stored in a structure optimized for querying and data analysis as a data warehouse. In that data warehouse, Table designs and their dimensions should be consistent throughout the time so that reports can be generated without disturbing the performance or the stability of the production systems. A data warehouse is a collection of data specific to the entire organization. On the other way data warehouse is collection of historical database from different functions within a company. Various definitions have been described of the data warehouse.

"A data warehouse is a database designed to support decision making in an organization".

or

"A data warehouse is a subject-oriented, integrated, time variant, and non-

volatile collection of data in support of management's decision-making process."

● **Subject-Oriented:** A data warehouse is organized around major subject, such as customer, product and sales. That is, data and information are organized according to a subject instead of an application. For example, data warehouses are on particular subjects like sales of product last few months or production of a product in the manufacturing department, etc., to analyze the past data.

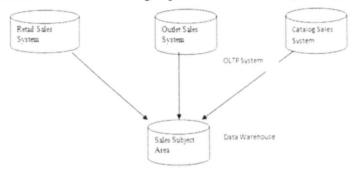

Figure 6.1: Subject-Oriented Sales Information

● **Non-volatile:** A data warehouse is always a physically separated store of data. Due to this separation, data warehouse does not require transaction processing, recovery, concurrency control, etc.

Data is stable in a data warehouse. More data is added, but data is never removed. It does not require transaction processing, recovery, and concurrency control mechanisms. It requires only two operations in data accessing:

● **Integrated:** A data warehouse is usually constructed by integrating multiple, heterogeneous sources, such as relational databases and flat files. The database contains data from most or all of an organization's operational applications, and these data are made consistent.

For example, in the above system like in Figure 6.1, the retail system uses a numeric 7-digit code for products, the outlet system code consists of 9 alphanumerics, and the catalog system uses 4 alphabets and 4 numerics. To create a useful subject area, the source data must be integrated. There is no need to change the coding in these systems, but there must be some mechanism to modify the data coming into the data warehouse and assign a common coding scheme.

OLTP Systems

Retail Sales System	Outlet Sales System	Catalog Sales System
Product code:	Product code:	Product code:
9999999	XXXXXXXXX	XXXX99.99
Product code		
Common code or a mapping of the various source codes		
Sales Subject Area		

- **Time-variant:** The data are stored in a data warehouse is to provide a historical perspective.Thus, the data in the data warehouse is time-variant or historical in nature. The data in the warehouse is 5 to 10 years old, or older, and are used for comparisons, trend analysis and forecasting. The changes to the data in the data warehouse are tracked and recorded so that reports can be produced showing the changes over time.

6.1.1 Need of the data warehouse

- Data integration
- Contains historical data
- Data is available but not information – and not the right information at the right time
- Set of new concept and important tools
- Advanced reporting and analysis
- Knowledge discovery and decision support
- Performance of fixed and adhoc queries is efficient
- Lots of new terms: ROLAP, MOLAP, HOLAP, rollup, drill-down, slice and dice have been introduced.
- Two types of applications: Operational applications and Analytical applications

Test Your Progress

1. Define data warehouse and its importance.
2. Why is a data warehouse constructed?
3. Why is data warehouse needed?
4. Compare data warehouse and database system.

6.1.2 Difference between Database and Data Warehouse

Table 1: Summarizes the Difference between Database and Data Warehouse

S.No.	Database	Data Warehouse
1	It is a collection of data organized for storage, accessibility, and retrieval.	It is a type of database that integrates data from various source systems and analyze them to create reports.
2	Use OLTP technique.	Use OLAP technique.
3	Modification of the database is continuous	Modification of data warehouse is in regular interval.
4	This records the data from the user for history.	This reads the historical data for the Users for business intelligence
5	Entity – Relational (E-R) modeling techniques are used for database design.	Data–Modeling techniques are used for the data warehouse design.

6	Designed to optimize for write operation.	Designed to optimize for read operations.
7	Performance is low for analysis queries.	High performance for analytical queries.
8	Cheaper to maintain.	Expensive to maintain.
9	Tables and joins are complex since they are normalized for **RDMS** (Relational Database Management System).It reduces redundant data.	Tables and joins are simple since they are de-normalized. It reduces the response time of query processing.

6.1.3 Benefits of Data Warehouse

Following are the benefits of data warehouse:

- Efficiently manage data and analyze them when files are scattered.
- A data warehouse is most suitable for aggregated queries on large amounts of data.
- Data warehouse architecture easily handles many transactions and understand many queries.
- Complex queries with normalized databases can be easier to create and maintain data warehouses, decreasing the workload on transaction systems.
- It is useful to manage various information from the number of users. It provides the capability to analyze historical data that gives a competitive advantage to the business.
- One of the best ways to data warehouse is to integrate data from multiple sources, enabling a central view across the enterprise.
- Due to integrated data single query engine can be used to present data.It supports decision support queries easier too.
- Because of being different from operational system, a data warehouse helps in retrieving data without showing down the operational system.
- Data warehouses enhance the value of operational business application like Customer Relationship Management (CRM) systems.
- Results draw in a variety of formats like reports, graphs, etc.
- Data warehouse provides efficient results in a very low computing cost.

6.1.4 Data Warehouse Applications

Data warehouse helps the business executives to organize, analyze and use their data for decision making. It is widely used in the following fields:

1. Financial services
2. Banking services
3. Consumer goods
4. Retail sectors

5.   Controlled manufacturing

6.   Agriculture

7.   Automobile

8.   Weather forecasting

6.1.5 Problems in Data Warehouse

1.   Underestimation of resources of data loading

2.   Preparation may be time consuming

3.   Required data not captured

4.   Increased end-user demands

5.   Hidden problems with source systems

6.   Data homogenization

7.   Data ownership

8.   High demand for resources

9.   High maintenance

10. Long-duration projects

11. Complexity of integration

12. Optimization

13. Warehouse maintenance: Schema design, initial loading and in metadata management

14. Extraction

15. Compatibility with existing system

16. Security issues

Test Your Progress

1.   Explain the problem and applications of data warehouse.

2.   Explain the benefits of data warehouse.

6.1.6 Basic Elements of Data Warehouse

Elements of data warehousing are divided into four categories which is shown in Figure 6.2.

1.   **Data Source:** Organization stores data into various databases divided up by the systems. These data may be sales data, marketing data, forecasting data, income tax data or any data which are useful for any organization. This data is stored in the form of operational data sources and Operational Data Store (ODS).

2.   **Staging:** It is an interface between operational source system and presentation area. Main purpose of staging is to combine, clean, transform and prepare source data for use in a data warehouse from the multiple sources. This data need not be based on relational terminology. In this stage various types of function has to be done by different managers like load manager performs the extraction and loading of data in the data warehouse; warehouse manager performs all the

operations related to the management like data aggregation, indexing, view, etc., and query manager retrieve the answer through queries which is done directly on the appropriate table, basically it is a backend component.

3.   **Data Presentation:** The presentation area actually constitutes data warehouse and data marts. Basically, it is a targeted machine where the data warehouse is organized and store for direct querying which is done by end users, report writers. Data warehouse divided into various data marts depending on the functions of business like investment data mart, sales data mart, etc.

4.   **Data access tools:** End user data access tools are any clients of the data warehouse. It can be categorized by reporting and query tools, application development tools, data mining tool, adhoc query tool, OLAP tool.

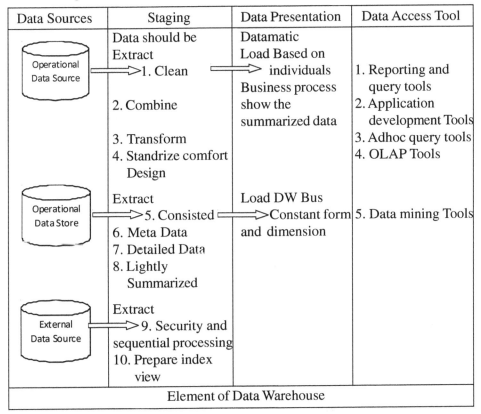

Data Sources	Staging	Data Presentation	Data Access Tool
Operational Data Source	Data should be Extract 1. Clean 2. Combine 3. Transform 4. Standrize comfort Design	Datamatic Load Based on individuals Business process show the summarized data	1. Reporting and query tools 2. Application development Tools 3. Adhoc query tools 4. OLAP Tools
Operational Data Store	Extract 5. Consisted 6. Meta Data 7. Detailed Data 8. Lightly Summarized	Load DW Bus Constant form and dimension	5. Data mining Tools
External Data Source	Extract 9. Security and sequential processing 10. Prepare index view		
Element of Data Warehouse			

Figure 6.2: Elements of Data Warehousing

Test Your Progress

1.   What is staging?
2.   Explain the basic elements of data warehousing.

6.2   Data Warehouse Architecture

In this section, various fundamental architecture properties have been discussed, these are:

1. **Separation:** Analytical and transaction processing should be kept apart as much as possible.

2. **Scalability:** Data warehouse architecture should be in scalable nature; means according to user's requirement upgrade and manage hardware and software.

3. **Extensibility:** In the context of data warehouse, extensibility means system can use new technologies and create new applications without redesign the whole system.

4. **Security:** Monitoring accesses are essential because of the strategic data stored in data warehouses.

5. **Administerability:** Data warehouse management should not be overly difficult.

Data warehouse architecture depends upon the organization's situation. There are three common typed of data warehouse architectures:

1. Basic architecture (single-level) of data warehouse.
2. Two-level architecture of data warehouse.
3. Three-level architecture of data warehouse.

6.2.1 Basic Architecture

Single layer architecture is a basic architecture of data warehouse which is not frequently used.In this architecture which is shown in Figure 6.3, end users can access data directly from the various source systems through the data warehouse. The goal of this architecture is to minimize the amount of data stored and remove the data redundancies.

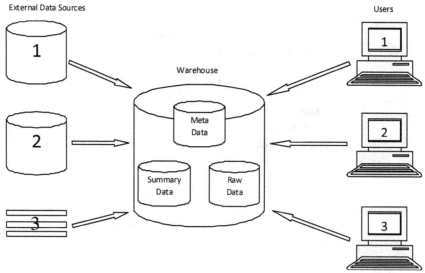

Figure 6.3: Basic Architecture of Data Warehouse

This architecture has one drawback, it fails when the separation between transaction processing and analytically takes place. Middleware interprets before analysis of queries are submitted to operational data. By this method regular transactional workloads are affected by queries. This architecture cannot log more data than sources, except the requirement of integration and correctness of data. Virtualization approach to data warehouse only successful when analysis needs are particularly restricted and the data volume to analyze is huge.

6.2.2 Two-level Architecture

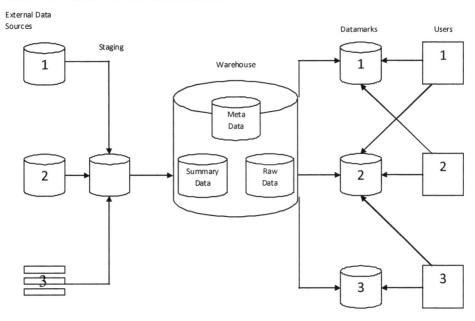

Figure 6.4: Two-level Architecture of Data Warehouse

Figure 6.4 shows two-level architecture of data warehouse to highlight the separation of physically available sources and data warehouses. This separation process is important to clean and process operational data, basically it consists five stages as follows:

1. **Data source:** It is a heterogeneous source data, it might be operational data, flat files, ODS etc.

2. **Staging area:** In this area, data stored to sources should be extracted, cleansed to remove inconsistencies and fill gaps before the warehouse.

3. **Warehouse:** It is a centralized repository which can access data directly, but it can also be used as a source for creating data marts.

4. **Data Marts:** Data mart is a partially copy of organization's data and is designed for a specific purpose like purchasing, sales, inventory, etc.

5. **Users:** End users can access the processed report, analyze them and mine them.

There is some difference between 2-tier and 3-tier architectures. They are as follows:

1. 2-tier architecture has only client and server whereas 3-tier architecture must consist middle-tier in between client and server.

2. Performance of 3-tier architecture is better than the 2-tier architecture because middle-tier query response is fast when 2-tiered architecture fail.

3. Scalability of 3-tier architecture is greater than the 2-tier architecture.

4. In 2-tier architecture, application and data reside on server because server has more disk space and processing power but in the 3-tier architecture data and applications are divided into database server and application server.

6.2.3 Three-layer Architecture:

In real-time, any organization generally adopts three layers (three-tier) architecture of data warehouse which is shown in Figure 6.5 is separated as bottom, middle and top tiers. These three tiers are described as:

Bottom-Tier: The bottom-tier of the architecture is the data warehouse database server that is almost a relational database system. In this layer, we extract the data from external sources or from operational databases into the bottom-tier.

Middle-Tier: Middle-tier is an OLAP server. It represents the output of query from a data warehouse or data marts. It is implemented using ROLAP (Relational OLAP) and MOLAP (multidimensional OLAP). ROLAP presents data in relational tables whereas MOLAP presents data in an array based structures means map directly to the data cube array structure.

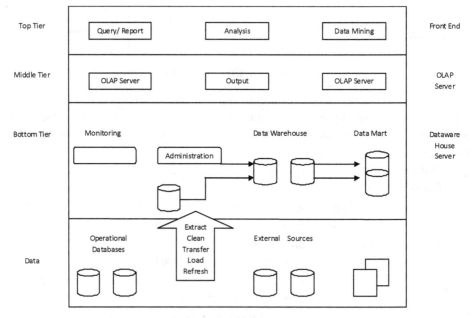

Figure 6.5: Three-tier Architecture of Data Warehouse

Top-Tier: It is a front end client layer which has various reporting tools, analysis tools and data mining tools for analysis behavior, prediction, generate report of last three months of an organization etc.

Test Your Progress

1. Explain the architecture of data warehouse.
2. Explain the three-level architecture of data warehouse.
3. Differentiate 2-tier and 3-tier architecture.

6.3 Data Mart

Data mart is a subset of a data warehouse and focused on a particular region, business unit and business function. They contain a subset of rows and columns which require by particular business. For example, a large organization which is at Delhi has some regional offices like in Bhopal, Indore, Jabalpur have their own data marts and they must contribute to the master data warehouse when it is needed at Delhi. Data marts do not normally contain detailed operational data, unlike data warehouse, so it is easy to understand and navigate than a data warehouse. Size of data marts is about 100 GB where as the data warehouse size varies 100 GB-TB.

Advantage

- Lower cost to build a datamart.
- It takes very less time to implement
- They are controlled individually rather than centrally.
- Each data mart has own decision support systems without relying on anyone else.
- It reduces network traffic to spread the query load into various data marts.
- To improve end-user response time due to the reduction in the volume of data accesses.
- Data cleaning,loading ,transformation and integration are far easier because it uses less data.

Disadvantage

- If size of the data mart increase performance will be decreased.
- Administration of multiple data marts becomes difficult.
- The problems in building and implementing multiple data marts arise.

6.3.1 Classification of Data Marts

Data marts are basically of two types: dependent data mart and independent data mart. Data mart is either dependent or independent; depends on the source of data.

(a)   Dependent Data Mart

Data can be derived from an enterprise-wide data warehouse. Data marts populated with data sourced from the enterprise data warehouse are known as dependent data marts. These data marts are also known as replicated data mart since the data mart is populated with a portion of the data warehouse's data through replication.

Data warehouse must consist of atomic level data, historical data, summarized data, data in multi-dimension. Queries and applications can access data from multi dimensional table or from relational dataset. Figure 6.6 shows the architecture for dependent marts:

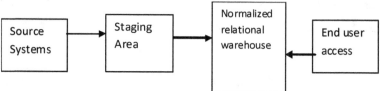

Figure 6.6: The Centralized Data Warehouse Architecture

(b)   Independent Data Mart

Independent data mart can collect data directly from the different sources.An organizational unit create its own data marts and each data mart would be independent of each other and whenever it will combine to fulfill its need, it does not provide "a single version of truth".These data marts have inconsistent data with different dimensions and measures that create difficulty to analyze data across the marts. Figure 6.7 shows the architecture for independent data marts.

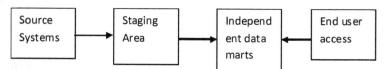

Figure 6.7 : The Independent Data Marts Architecture

Test Your Progress

1.   Explain the importance of data mart in data mining.

2.   Classify the data marts.

3.   What are the advantages of disadvantages of data marts?

6.3.2 Steps for implementation of Data Mart

There are five basic steps for implementing the data marts.

Step-1: Design the Schema

It performs following tasks:

1.   Collect information about the organization and technical requirements.

2.   Find out data sources.

3.   Select a data subset which is useful for any organization.

4.   Design logical and physical structure of data mart.

Step-2: Constructing physical storage

It performs following tasks:

1. Create physical database and storage structure (for example, table spaces related to the data mart).
2. Create schema objects (for example, tables and indexes defined in the design step).
3. Determining how best to set up the tables and the access structures.

Step-3: Populating the data mart from source system

It performs following tasks:

1. Mapping source data to target data structure.
2. Extracting data.
3. Cleansing and transformation of data.
4. Loading data.
5. Creating and storing metadata.

Step-4: Accessing the data

It performs following tasks:

1. Data can access for query, analysis, reports, charts and graphs.
2. Translates database structure and objects name into business terms so that end user can interact with the data mart easily.
3. Setup and manage database structure.

Step-5: Managing over its lifetime

It performs following tasks:

1. Secure access of data.
2. Optimize the system for better performance.
3. Increase the growth of data.
4. Fault tolerant.

Test Your Progress

1. How to implement data mart in data mining?

6.4　Multidimensional Data Models

To describe the multidimensional data models there are three types of schemas defined:These are star schema, snowflake schema and fact constellations. A schema is a collection of database objects, including tables, views and indexes.

6.4.1　Star Schema

Star schema or sometimes called star join schema is defined as a relational database schema. It is a simple style of database schema. As a name suggested Star, means it consist one fact table in the middle connected to multiple dimension tables and arrange like a Star.

Figure 6.8 shows the basic template of Star schema with one fact table that is sales table which have foreign keys, whereas store, time, customer and product are multiple dimension tables with descriptive, hierarchical attributes.

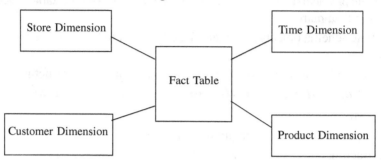

Figure 6 8: Template of Star Schema

Figure 6.9 shows another example shows the star schema for a drug with descriptive and hierarchical attributes.

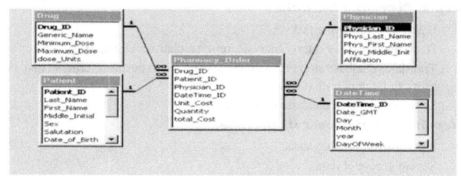

Figure 6.9: AExample of Star Schema

Advantages

1.   Fast inquiry processing.
2.   We can easily controlled varying anomalies because in the case of classification no sudden changes required.
3.   Simple and intuitive data model.
4.   High traceability and comprehensibility.
5.   Slicing Down.
6.   Supported by a large number of business intelligent tools.
7.   Performance increase.
8.   Direct mapping.

Disadvantages

1.   Less memory utilization.

2. Dimension table does not have parent table.

3. Redundancy of data into multiple dimension table.

4. Data access latency is less due to highly denormalize of data.

5. Creation of aggregation is difficult.

6.4.2 Snowflake Schema

Snowflake schema is an extension of the star schema by normalizing dimension tables. Normalization is basically splitting data to avoid redundancy.It is generally used when a dimension table is lengthy.To understand this big dimension table, add sub-tables into each dimension table.The effect of snowflaking affects only dimension tables and not the fact table.

Figure 6.10 shows the basic template of Snowflake schema with centralized sales fact table connected to multiple dimension tables like store,time,customer and product with its normalize form.

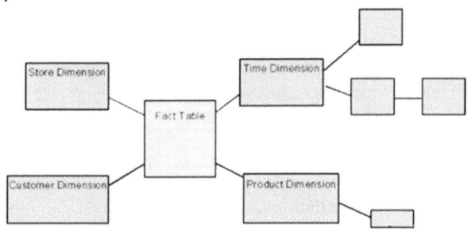

Figure 6.10: Template of Snowflake Schema

Figure 6.11 shows the another example which shows the snowflake schema for a drug with normalized multidimensional table to reduce redundancy.

Advantages

1. Data redundant means occupy less space.

2. Easy to update and maintained by normalized property.

3. It provides greater flexibility in interrelationship between dimension levels and components.

4. Data access latency is high.

5. Easy to understand by join multiple dimensions.

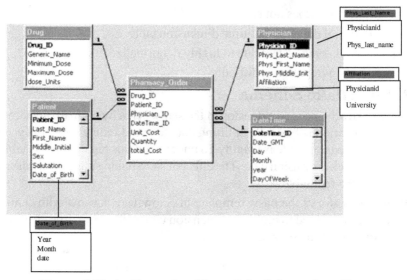

Figure 6.11: An Example of Snowflake Schema for a Drug

Disadvantages

1. Additional maintenance efforts needed due to the increase number of lookup tables.

2. Due to the higher number of joins between dimension tables and then to fact table; performance is low.

3. There are More complex queries and hence difficult to understand.

4. Content browsing is difficult.

6.4.3 Fact Constellations

As a name suggests its shape like a constellation of stars, i.e., star schema. Fact constellation is also known as galaxy schema because it is a collection of star schemas which shares their dimension.It is dissimilar to star and snowflake schema in terms of multiple fact tables.This allows dimension table to be shared amongst the fact tables.Fact constellation limits the possible queries for the warehouse.

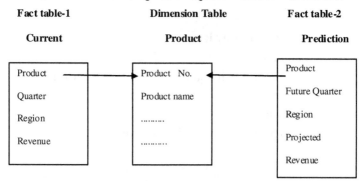

Figure 6.12: Example of Fact Constellation

Figure 6.12 shows a fact constellation with two fact tables, current production and prediction.These share the dimension table product.

Test Your Progress

1. What is schema?
2. Explain the types of schema in data warehouse.
3. What are the advantages and disadvantages of various schemas in data warehouse?

6.5   Summary

This Chapter discussed about theneed of data warehouse, elements of data warehouse, problems associated to data warehouse,architecture and their comparison, data models and classification of data models.

6.6   Key Terms

● **Data mart**: The access layer of the data warehouse environment that is used to get data out to the users.

● **Data warehouse:** A database designed to support decision making in an organization.

● **Middleware:**The software layer that lies between the operating system and the applications on each side of a distributed computer network.

● **Star schema**: The simplest style of data mart schema.

6.7   Exercise

1. What is a data warehouse? Discuss the basic characteristics of a data warehouse.
2. Differentiate 2-tier and 3-tier architecture.
3. What are the different types of data mart?
4. Define data cube. How can we convert tables and spreadsheets to data cubes?
5. Differentiate between star and snowflake schema.
6. Describe the 3-tier data warehouse architecture.
7. Explain problem associated with data warehouse.
8. Explain the need of a data warehouse.

University Questions

1. What is Data Warehouse? **[UPTU 2013-14]**What are the characteristics or features? **[UPTU 2006-07, 2008-09, 2009-10]**

   Refer section 6.1 and 6.1.1 and 6.1.3

2. Explain the three-Tier warehouse Architecture.
   [UPTU 2004-05, 2008-09, 2010-11,2013-14]

   Refer section 6.2.3

3. What is a Data Mart? **[UPTU 2012-13,2013-14]**

Explain its role in datawarehousing.How is a data mart difference from data warehouse?   **[UPTU 2006-07, 2010-11]**

Refer section 6.3

4.   Describe the star, snowflake and fact constellationsschemas for multidimensional database.   **[UPTU 2009-2010, 2010-11, 2011-12, 2012-13]**

Refer section 6.4

5.   Differentiate database and data warehouse.   **[UPTU 2013-14]**

Refer section 6.1.2

Unit-5

Aggregation, Historical information, Query Facility, OLAP function and Tools. OLAPServers, ROLAP, MOLAP, HOLAP, Data Mining interface, Security, Backup andRecovery, Tuning Data Warehouse, Testing Data Warehouse.

Chapter 7
OLAP Technology

7.1 Overview of OLAP System

"OLAP (Online Analytical Processing) is method to organize and analyze metadata from multidimensional database to support business intelligence."

Section 7.1.1 and Section 7.1.2 describe some basic terms of OLAP which are helpful to understand what OLAP is? Main motive of OLAP technology is basically used for analysis of previous and current database of any organization and takes fruitful decision for the organization on the basis of facts. A fact is an instance of some particular occurrence or event and the properties of the event all stored in a database it could be a count, sum or average of the order amounts. OLAP divides those facts into multidimensions. Basically OLAP technology consists of multidimensional databases and aggregation.

Test Your Progress

1. What is OLAP?
2. Write the main motive of OLAP technology.

7.1.1 Multidimensional Database

Multidimensional models are used to perform analysis of data rather than performing online transactions on data.Analysis on data is the main objective of developing data warehouses. It is used when it requires large amount of data for making decision. Various advantages of multidimensional database over two-dimensional database or relational database, such as based on organization's parameter an organization can compare their sales of months. This approach can also predict the selling of upcoming months which are shown as Figure 7.1.

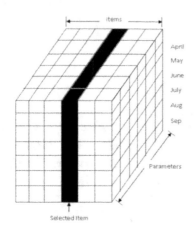

Parameters			
	Units	Cost	Profit
March	250	500	2%
April	450	700	5%
May	350	650	4%
June	450	690	7%
July	550	750	9%

Selected Item Analysis

Figure 7.1: An Example of Multidimensional Data Cube

OLAP database shows how various data cubes and individual cube are organized, and designed by a cube administrator in the way that you simply retrieve and analyze data which is also helpful for preparing PivotTable reports, charts, and graphs which you simply need.

The goal of multidimensional data model is to support analysis in simple and faster way to executive, managers and business professionals.

7.1.2 Aggregation

Aggregation is nothing but a technique to merge or consolidate dispersed data into a single data. The data that has been summarized is called the summarized data. Aggregation is done to speed up the query process and improve the overall performance in the term of query response time.

One disadvantage of aggregation is that although the queries are run faster so some data may be lost. Multidimensional databases usually have hierarchies or fact-based relationships of data from each dimension. Aggregation calculates all the data relationships from each data cube's dimensions, For example, a set of buyers can be grouped by urban, by district or by rural; so accompanying 50 cities, 8 wards plus twin countries there are trinity hierarchical stages beside 60 divisions. These buyers can be considered in relation to merchandises; if there are 250 produces beside 20 categories, three families and three departments then there are 276 product members. Accompanying even these pair sizes there are 16,560 (276 * 60) workable groups. As the data raises, number of aggregations can also raise. Aggregation makes direct effect on the OLAP server CPU(Central Processing Unit) usage, cube build time, cube file size query response time and file I/O(Input/Output).

The terms data warehousing and online analytical processing are used interchangeably. These apply to different components of systems referred to as decision support systems or business intelligence systems. For example, suppose a market analyst wants to get a yearly progress graph of an organization to find recent trends based on aggregated data. Business intelligence is the process of extracting data from an OLAP database to analyze that data and information which are useful for making informed business decisions and take action accordingly. Decision support system or business intelligence would help to answer the following questions:

- How do the yearly sale of any product to another year of selling?
- How will our profit on this year compare with identical period of time throughout the last past years?
- Which salesperson, distributors, vendors are not good for our business?
- Customers respond for any product in this year and last month/year.
- What is the breakdown profitability?

Test Your Progress

1. Explain multidimensional database.
2. How aggregation performs in database?

7.2 OLAP Tools

Aim of OnLine Analytical Processing (OLAP) tool is used to analyze multidimensional data interactively from multiple perspectives. It is different from the ETL (Extract-Transform-Load) tool as in ETL tools are used to store the data in a target tables firstly extract the data from multiple sources and then apply transformations on them to achieve the standard of business and business logic. On the other hand OLAP tools load the data extracted and located by ETL tool then make the report using these tables.

OLAP have three basic analytical operations, such as consolidation (roll-up), drill-down, and slicing and dicing, which are described as follows:

1. Consolidation/Roll up

The Consolidation or Roll up operation is also called **Drill-up operation**. It involves the aggregation of data by complex grouping of inter-related data. The operation performs aggregation on data cube is done by either climbing up a concept hierarchy or by dimension reduction. Figure 7.2 (b) represents a rollup operation

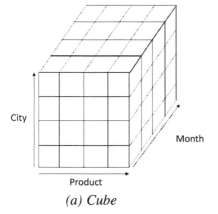

(a) Cube

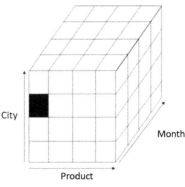

(b) Rollup operation of figure (a)

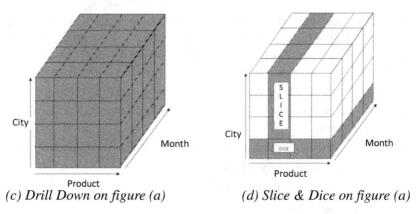

(c) Drill Down on figure (a)   *(d) Slice & Dice on figure (a)*

Figure 7.2: Basic Analytical Operations

simplification of Figure 7.2(a). Here Instead of looking at one single fact considers all the facts from multidimensional cube.

Another example of Roll-up operation is also shown in Figure 7.3.

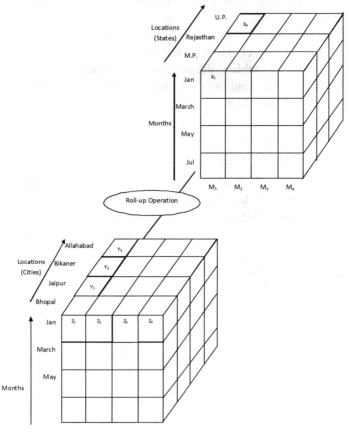

Figure 7.3: Example of Roll-up Operation

- Roll-Up operation is used the concept of hierarchy.
- Equivalent to doing GROUP BY to this dimension by using attribute hierarchy.
- Initially the concept hierarchy was arranged in "street < city < province < country".
- On rolling up the data is aggregated by ascending the location hierarchy from the level of city to level of country.
- By this operation besides of countries data are grouped into cities.
- After the roll-up operation one or more dimension will be removed from the data cube.

2.   Drill-Down

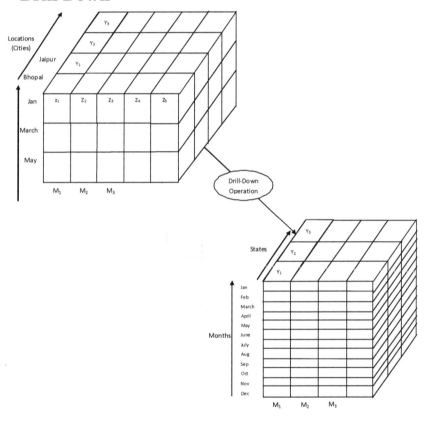

Figure 7.4: Example of Drill-Down Operation

Drill-Down is also called roll down by having the reverse features of Roll-Up operation of OLAP Cube. Figure 7.2(c) represents a drill-down operation simplification of Figure 7.2(a). This operation may introduce new dimensions for understanding summarized (i.e., up) data to the most detailed (i.e., down).Operation performed by either introduces new dimension or delete one or more dimensions using the concept hierarchy. In short drill-down operation appears as single unit within a specific area of each of the dimension. You can also understand Drill-down operation in more detail by Figure 7.4

Following are the features of Drill-down operation:

● Drill-down is just the opposite to roll up. Drill down goes from higher-level details to lower-level details.

● At the starting phase the hierarchy concept was arranged as "day<month<quater<year."

● On drill-up the time dimension is descended from the level quarter to the level of month.

● During the Drill-down operation one or more dimensions from the data cube are added.

● It proposes highly detailed data from less detailed data.

3.   Slice

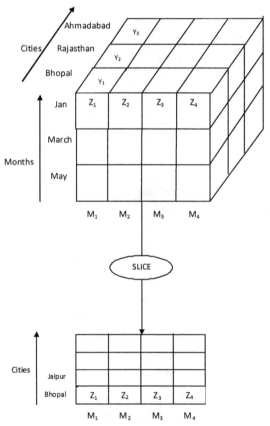

Figure 7.5: A Example of Slice Operation

This operation is used for searching and accessing data in the cube by selecting a one dimension on a cube and proposed a new sub-cube. It reduces the dimensionality of the cubes. Figure 7.2(d) gives a simplification of Slice operation on Figure 7.2(a). Another example is also defined in Figure 7.5, in which Slice operation is performed for the dimension month using the criterion month ="Jan".

Consider the Figure 7.5, which shows the Slice operation.

4.   DICE

The Dice operation performs selection of two or more dimension on a given cube and gives us a new subcube. It reduces the number of member values of one or more dimensions. This can be performed by a Slice operation on one dimension and then rotating the cube to select on a second dimension. Figure 7.2(d) also shows the basic operation of Dice on Figure 7.2(a) parallel to Slice Operation. You can also understand this operation by selecting following criteria that involve three dimensions which is shown in Figure 7.6.

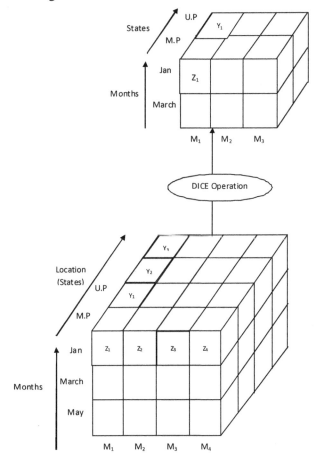

Figure 7.6: A Example of Slice Operation

● (location = "MP" or "UP")

- (month= "jan" or "march")
- (item =" M1" or "M2" or "M3").

5.   Pivot

This operation is used when a user wishes to change the direction or orientation of the view of the cube. In this operation, position of some columns or rows may be changed. This is also known as **rotation.** Figure 7.7 describing the Pivot operation.

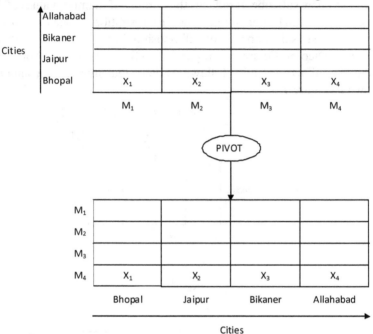

Figure 7.7: Example of Pivot Operation

Test Your Progress

1. Explain basic operations of OLAP.
2. Why is slice operation used?

7.3   Difference between Online Transaction Processing and Online Analytical Processing

Online Transaction Processing System (OLTP) and Online Analytical Processing system (OLAP) are the two basic activities of database and these are correlated to each other. In a practical life day-to-day transactions would be the source data to the data warehouse, after that OLAP system helps to analyze it, this correlation is described in Figure 7.8.

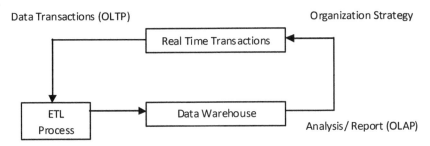

Figure 7.8: Correlation of OLAP and OLTP Processes

We have already discussed about OLAP technology in Section 7.1.Now, we turn to know the basics about Online Transaction Processing (OLTP).This processing system is characterized by a large number of current online transaction commands like INSERT,DELETE,UPDATE, etc. For example in a banking System, you withdraw amount through an ATM (Automated Teller Machine). Then account Number; in that case ATM PIN Number, Amount you are withdrawing and balance amount are operational data elements. It also maintains data integrity of multi-environment and effectiveness in terms of transaction per second.

Table 7.1 summarizes the major differences between OLTP and OLAP system design.

Table 7.1: Difference between OLTP and OLAP Activity

Key Features	OLTP	OLAP
Customers	IT Professional, Clerk, Businessman,students, etc.	Person Analyser, Knowledge Worker, etc.
Basic Resources	Active Data (Current and original data),Operational database	Integrated by various OLTP databases, Analyzed data
Function Used	Day-to-day Operation	Decision Support System
Database Design	Purpose-Oriented	Subject-Oriented
Motive	Frequently execute basic and business level task	Analyze from multidimen-sional datasets, Take right decision for future prediction, Planning, Problem Solving
Transactions	Very short and frequent transaction.For example, withdraw amount from ATM, Filling Shopping Cart, etc.	Long Transaction, Complex queriesFor example, Analysis of population, Best sale, etc.
Procedure	Repetitive ad-hoc	

Processing Speed	Typically very fast less than 1 second	It depends on Complexity of query and size of data
Database Capacity	Less than GB	More than GB
No. of Users	Every people use in our real life	Less people can use like analyzer
Workload	Predefined, i.e., already decided	Unforeseeable, i.e., not able to be predicted.

Test Your Progress

1. Compare OLAP and OLTP.
2. Name some of the online transaction commands.

7.4   OLAP Server

Online Analytical Processing (OLAP) is a new technology, to perform multi-dimensional analysis of datasets and provides the capabilities for complex calculations, trend analysis, planning, forecasting and simulation modelling using OLAP server. If an organization wants their annual benefits there must be a client and server.

The main component of OLAP is the OLAP server. OLAP server sits between a client and database management system. OLAP server understands the organization of data in the database. It supports the data types like text, numeric, string date and multimedia data types like images sound. OLAP server contains a large number of aggregate functions that are used for computations; Oracle Express Server and Hyperion Solutions Essbase are some popular predefined OLAP server software programs.

OLAP server basically categorized as:

1. Relational OLAP(ROLAP)
2. Multi-dimensional OLAP (MOLAP)
3. Hybrid OLAP (HOLAP)
4. Specialized SQL Server

Let us discuss each of them in brief.

1.   Relational OLAP (ROLAP)

ROLAP stands for Relational Online Analytical Processing.It is placed between relational back end server and client front end tools. ROLAP uses bottom up approach and uses Star schema data warehouse. ROLAP stores all data in multi-dimensional cube, including aggregations, in the source relational database. This type of storage is beneficial to organization that wants to create data warehouse. For directly interaction to data warehouse ROLAP uses an SQL reporting tool.

This methodology depends on manipulating the information in relational database using slicing and dicing function. Basically, every action of slicing and dicing is equivalent to adding a "WHERE" clause within the SQL statement.

ROLAP includes the following.

- Implementation of aggregation navigation logic.
- Optimization for each DBMS back end.
- Use function such as Slicing and dicing
- Additional tools and services.
- Handle non-aggregatable facts.

Figure 7.9 describes how ROLAP server works.

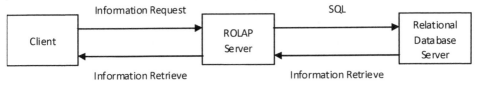

Figure 7.9: Process of ROLAP Server

Advantages

1. It can handle large amount of data.
2. Efficiently manage both numeric and textual data.
3. ROLAP tools are better in handling non-aggregatable facts.
4. It facilitates the feature authorization controls.
5. In ROLAP server data are stored as relational database that can be accessed by SQL tools .
6. Low latency

Disadvantages

1. ROLAP applications display a slower performance as compared to other style of OLAP tools.
2. Some calculations are not translatable easily into SQL query; but ROLAP uses SQL for manipulation.
3. Direct access to cell.
4. Loading aggregate tables must follow basic extract, transform and loading scenario and ROLAP server does not support this task so that additional overhead the time and code.
5. It gives the poorest query performance because no objects benefit from multi-dimensional storage.

2. Multidimensional OLAP (MOLAP)

Multidimensional OLAP is the more traditional way of OLAP analysis. It extends OLAP functionality to MDBMS (Multidimensional Database Management System). Main difference between MOLAP against a ROLAP tool is that data are pre-summarized and are stored in a proprietary format in a multidimensional cube, instead of in a relational database. It uses top down approaches. In MOLAP, both source data and the aggregation calculations are stored in multidimensional cubes and these data cubes held in memory called "Cube Cache", so that data retrieval process is fast but it also required more storage for data and calculations. In that process, data is stored in the binary format. Whenever data cube will process; data inside the cube will refresh; in that case latency will be high. Basic process of MOLAP server is described in Figure 7.10.

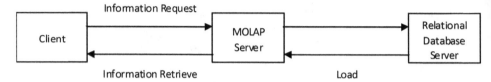

Figure 7.10: Process of MOLAP Server

Advantages

1. Faster indexing to pre-computed summarized data.
2. Automated computation of higher-level aggregates of the data.
3. One of the advantages of MOLAP is that all complex calculations not only solved but they return quickly.
4. It provides compress data so less space is required.
5. Array models provide natural indexing.
6. Pre-structuring of aggregated data achieves effective data extraction.

Disadvantages

1. It can handle limited amount of data since calculations are pre-defined in the cube.
2. Newly inserted data will not be available for analysis until the cube is processed.
3. Some MOLAP introduces data redundancy.
4. It supports limited set of queries.
5. It suffers from very high cardinality (dimensions).
6. Difficult to update query models with more than ten dimensions; it also depends on complexity and cardinality of dimensions.

3.   Hybrid OLAP (HOLAP)

The hybrid OLAP approach combines the features of ROLAP and MOLAP servers into a single architecture with greater scalability of ROLAP and the faster computation of MOLAP. In short, this tool provides the features of Multi-Dimensional DataBase (MDDB) and Relational Database Management System (RDBMS) both, which is shown in Figure 7.11. For example, HOLAP systems store larger quantities of detailed data in the relational tables while the aggregations are stored in the pre-calculated cubes. One of the advantages of HOLAP is "drill through" capability from the cube down to the relational tables for described data. Some advantages of HOLAP tool are efficient data processing, flexible to data accessing and better scalability.

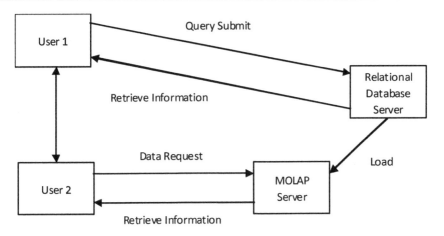

Figure 7.11: Process of HOLAP Server

4. Specialized SQL Server

Motive of specialized SQL servers is to provide query processing support for SQL queries and provide advanced query language in star and snowflake schemas with a read-only environment.

There are also some types of OLAP servers which are still not much popular described here:

(i) Spatial OLAP (SOLAP)

SOLAP integrates Geographic Information System (GIS) and OLAP into a single system to handle both spatial and non-spatial data, means data is not only in an alphanumeric form but also in image and vectors.

(ii) Mobile OLAP (MOLAP)

Mobile OLAP refers to the functionalities of OLAP on mobile device or any other wireless device. It is also called Remote OnLine Analytical Processes because OLAP data accesses remotely by wireless device. For example, ActivePivot, which allows accessing data and some capabilities through your smartphone, iPad, or any other mobile device.

(iii) Desktop OLAP (DOLAP)

Desktop OLAP is also known by Local OLAP, can download the data locally or within the desktop and after that processed it. Some DOLAP products allow only read access. DOLAP is easy to implement but with limited functionality. Its cost is also very less as compares to other OLAP applications.

DOLAP database is achieved by a central server or processing routine that prepares data cubes for every user, after that each user can then access their portion of the data.

(iv)   Web-based OLAP (WOLAP)

WOLAP is another type of OLAP server which accesses the OLAP data through Web browser using 3-tiered architecture. 3-tier architecture consist three components: a client, a middleware and a server. This WOLAP invests lower cost and enhances the accessibility of data, as there are lower deployment costs and all a user needs in an Internet connection and Web browser. But still it is not compare to a conventional client/server machine.

Test Your Progress

1.   What is OLAP server?
2.   Differentiate various types of OLAP servers.
3.   Compare MOLAP and HOLAP.
4.   What is Mobile OLAP?
5.   Write the features of Web-based OLAP.

7.5   Applications of OLAP:

OLAP is commonly used in various fields of database management system, various applications had to be developed that would be helpful for taking right decisions for their organization.There are some applications categorized as:

● Financial Applications
● Activity-based costing or in resource allocation
● Budgeting
● Financial services industry (Banks, insurance, etc.)
● Marketing/sales applications
● Market research analysis
● Sales forecasting
● Promotions analysis
● Customer analysis
● Customer segmentation
● Business modeling
● Simulating business behavior
● Find right decision for managers
● Database marketing
● Server management and data integration
● Vision enterprises EssInfo
● Hyperion integration server
● Sybase power designer

7.6   Benefits of OLAP

OLAP holds several benefits for businesses:

1. OLAP data are reliable, consistent, and its calculation is also very easy and fast.
2. OLAP views multi-dimensional data; it helps managers to take profitable decision for their organization.
3. It is particularly useful when comparing information from previous years/month to information contain in current year/month and prepares graph analysis.
4. OLAP applications are self-sufficient due to the inherent flexibility provided to the organized databases.
5. OLAP is helpful in faster information retrieval, application backlog and reduction in query drag.
6. It provides single platform in terms of information, planning, business needs, forecasting, reporting, budgeting and analysis.
7. Multi-dimensional presentation will produce an understanding of relationships not previously realized.

Test Your Progress

1. Describe the applications of OLAP.
2. Explain the various benefits of OLAP which are useful in data warehouse.

7.7 Processing of OLAP queries

The idea about index is to give pointers to the rows in a table with its key value for efficient data accessing. This should be achieved by storing identities (IDs) of each row for each key. In this Section, we describe how to index OLAP data by different indexing techniques.

(i) **B-Tree Index:** Two representations (rowid and bitmap) are implemented at the leaves of the index depending on the cardinality of the data. Most of commercial products are Oracle, Informix, Red Brick.

Advantages

*   Fast processing.
*   Suited for high cardinality.
*   Space requirement is independent of the cardinality of the indexed column.
*   Cost is not effective in case of updated indexed column since individual rows are locked.

Disadvantages

*   Inefficiently for low cardinality data.
*   Not support to adhoc queries.
*   The indexes cannot be combined before fetching the data.

(ii) **Pure Bitmap Index:** Every bits of an array is used to represent every distinct column value of every row in a table, setting the bits related to the row either 1 or 0. In this indexing technique equality encoding scheme is used. Most commercial products for this technique are Oracle, Informix, Sybase, Informix,

Red Brick, DB2.

Advantages

- Suitable for low cardinality columns.
- Perform bitwise operations.
- Indexes have to be combined for pointer before fetching raw data.
- Low space
- Also implemented in parallel machine too.
- Easy to build.
- Efficiently perform scalar functions.
- Easy to add new indexed value.
- Suitable for OLAP.

Disadvantages

- Inefficient for high cardinality data.
- Expensive to update index column. Another row cannot be updated until Whole bitmap segment of the Updated row will be released.
- Does not support spare data.

(iii) **Encoded Bitmap Index:** Encoded bitmap index is the binary Bit-Sliced Index which is built on the attribute domain. One of most popular example is DB2.

Advantages

- Uses space efficiently.
- Efficiently perform with wide range query.

Disadvantages

- It performs inefficiently with equality queries.
- Difficult to find a good encoding scheme.
- When a new indexed vale is added so encoded bitmap also be rebuilt instantly.

(iv) **Bitmap Join Index:** Bitmap join index is built with restriction of a column on the dimension table in the fact table. Most popular commercial product for this technique are Oracle, Informix, Red Brick.

Advantages

- Flexible.
- Efficient.
- Supports Star queries.

Disadvantages

Order of indexed column is important.

(v) **Projection Index:** The index is created through actual values of column(s) stored in indexed table. Most popular commercial product for this technique is Sybase.

Advantages

It speeds up the performance when a few columns in the table are retrieved.

Disadvantages

Main disadvantage is that it only retrieves raw data.

Test Your Progress

1. Explain bitmap join index, and its advantages and disadvantages.
2. How OLAP query processes?

7.8 Data Mining Interfaces

Data mining interfaces basically used to mine datasets from Database Management System (DBMS); it is one of the important features in data mining.

These are primary interfaces that are used to mine data from DBMS.

1. Report Generators
2. Views
3. QBE (Query-By-Example) Tools
4. SQL(Structured-Query-Language)

Report Generators

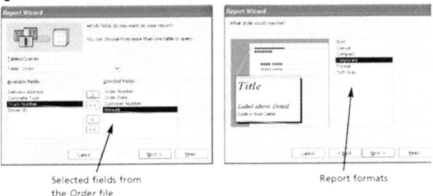

Selected fields from
the *Order* file

Report formats

Figure7.12: Example of Report Generator using Report Wizard

Report generator as shown in Figure 7.12 helps us to generate quickly defined formats in which information are arranged as per your need. Theses report you can save on your disks and generate report whenever you want with updated information.

A report generator generally takes data from a source, such as a database (like Customer database) and uses it to produce a document (report) which satisfies the given condition (for example, a Customer and Amount report can either be generated as per a range of Order Dates or Amount wise or even indexed by a Customer Number filed) as shown in Figure 7.13.

CUSTOMER AND AMOUNT REPORT

Customer Number	Order Number	Order Date	Amount
1234	100000	9/1/2004	8
1234	100002	9/2/2004	6
1234	100006	9/5/2004	4
1234	100009	9/7/2004	8
1234	100015	9/12/2004	8
2345	100007	9/6/2004	5
2345	100012	9/9/2004	8
3456	100001	9/1/2004	3
4567	100003	9/3/2004	4
4567	100004	9/4/2004	8
4567	100011	9/9/2004	6
4567	100013	9/10/2004	4
5678	100005	9/4/2004	4
6789	100008	9/6/2004	8
6789	100010	9/9/2004	7
6789	100014	9/10/2004	6

Figure 7.13: Customer and Amount Report

Views

This is a command in DBMS that allows us to see the contents of database files as per our required formats and fields

This is just a view content of DBMS not an original files; you can make changes in these files and revert back to original database contents for required changes.

You can execute a query on views and perform simple sorting as per your requirements (see Figure 7.14). It is very similar to a workbook without any row numbers.

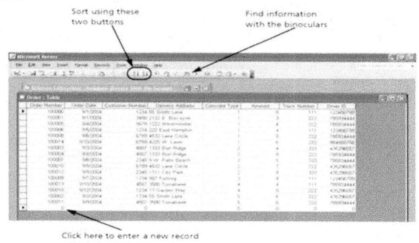

Figure 7.14: View the Datasheet

Query-By-Example (QBE) Tool

This data mining interface provides an answer of your questions in graphical form. For example, like "Namethe driver who most often delivers concrete triple a Home".

Query by Example (QBE) is a database query language for relational databases. It was introduced by Moshé M. Zloof at IBM (International Business Machines) Research during 1970s. It was the first widely used graphical query language, using visual tables where the user would enter commands, example elements and conditions. Figure 7.15 displays the result using QBE. QBE, with reference to Microsoft Access, is used to database querying. This feature is also used as a userfriendly database management system for small businesses.

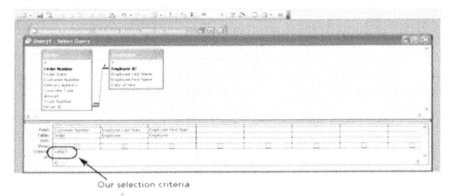

Our selection criteria

Customer Number	Employee Last Name	Employee First Name
4567	Evaraz	Antonio
4567	Robertson	John
4567	Robertson	John
4567	Robertson	John

; *Query-By-Example*

ition in DBMS. This also performs
that it uses structured sentences
ely used by IT persons.

very

ase; it is an environment which
nt and historical information to

his section focus on various ideas
that contribute towards data warehouse security.

1.   Replication Control

Replication can be viewed in a slightly different manner than perceive in traditional literature. For example, an old copy can be considered a replica of the current copy of the data. A slightly out-of-date data can be considered as a good substitute for some users. The basic idea is that either the warehouse keeps different replicas of the same items or creates them dynamically. The legitimate users get the most consistent and complete copy of data while casual users get a weak replica. Such replica may be enough to satisfy the user's need but do not provide information that can be used maliciously or breach privacy. We have formally defined the equivalence of replicas and this notion can be used to create replicas for different users. The replicas may be at one central site or can be distributed to proxies who may serve the users efficiently. In some cases, the user may be given the weak replica and may be given an upgraded replica if willing to pay or deserve it.

2.   Aggregation and Generalization

The concept of warehouse is based on the idea of using summaries and consolidators. This implies that source data is not available in raw form. This lends to ideas that can be used for security. Some users can get aggregates only over a large number of records whereas others can be given for small data instances. The granularity of aggregation can be lowered for genuine users. The generalization idea can be used to give users a high-level information at first but the lower level details can be given after the security constraints are satisfied. For example, the user may be given an approximate answer initially based on some generalization over the domains of the database. Inheritance is another notion that will allow increasing capability of access for users. The users can inherit access to related data after having access to some data item.

3.   Exaggeration and Misleading

These concepts can be used to mutilate the data. A view may be available to support a particular query, but the values may be overstated in the view. For security concern, quality of views may depend on the user involved and user can be given an exaggerated view of the data. For example, instead of giving any specific sales figures, views may scale up and give only exaggerated data. In certain situations warehouse data can give some misleading information; information which may be partially incorrect or difficult to verify the correctness of the information. For example, a view of a company's annual report may contain the net profit figure including the profit from sales of properties (not the actual sales of products).

4.   Anonymity

Anonymity is to provide user and warehouse data privacy. A user does not know the source warehouse for his/her query and warehouse also does not who is the user and what particular view a user is accessing (view may be constructed from many source databases for that warehouse). Note that a user must belong to the group of registered users and similarly, a user must also get data from only legitimate warehouses. In such cases, encryption is to be used to secure the connection between the users and warehouse so that no outside user (user who has not registered with the warehouse) can access the warehouse.

5.   User Profile-Based Security

User profile is a representation of the preferences of any individual user. User profiles can help in authentication and determining the levels of security to access warehouse data. User profile must describe how and what has to be represented pertaining to the users information and security level authorization needs. The growth in warehouses has made relevant information access difficult in reasonable time due to the large number of sources differ in terms of context and representation. Warehouse can use data category details in determining the access control. For example, if a user would like to access an unpublished annual company report, the warehouse server may deny access to it. The other alternative is to construct a view to reflect only projected sales and profit report. Such a construction of view may be transparent to the user. A server can use data given in the profile to decide whether the user should be given the access to associated graphical image data. The server has the option to reduce the resolution or later the quality of impages before making them available to users.

Despite of maintain data warehouse its **backup and recovery** is an important task, which aims to care of data centre, database and data mining and if failure occurs then it reconstructs or recovers by various recovery strategies.

Backup is a copy of original data to save data applications which is an important part of database, control file and any transaction processing applications. There are also various types of backups available on Oracle 7, depending on the business need of the system, such as:

● Logical Export

● Offline backup or cold database backup

● Online backup or hot database backup

Logical database backup can be handling with EXPORT command line provided by Oracle. **Logical export backup** is taken after the day of completion, aims to minimize the impact of online database processing. In logical export first, reads data from the database and copies each object from database into a binary format and after that this binary file is stored in a location defined by EXPORT command line parameters, and move the backup to tape. It takes logical backup using EXPORT tool; logical backup are very helpful to resolve user error. For this method data should be read inconsistent and non-changeable by any other transaction during the process. One drawback of this method is that it does not use archived redo logs.

Administrator can keep physical data during processing using 'Cold' and 'Hot' database backup. **Cold database backup or offline backup** is continuously backing up the entire data warehouse or database is closed which suffers a problem if there is limited space. In this method database should be shutdown using shutdown immediate statements and shutdown abort operations. These statements and operations are used to next time to be opened database that will be shutdown. DBA (Database Administrator) will take the replica of database when database is shutdown normally. These files are of four types, such as data files, control files, redo logs files and parameter files. Whereas **Hot database backing up** or **Online backing up**, data warehouses with databases and related files during its updation. It takes combinational view of logical and physical database and is also used to archiving redo logs to recover the backup. Basically online backup is an iterative process to be taken one tablespace at a time. In this process first, place the tablespace into a backup mode with the alter tablespace. Second, execute them, and after that administrator makes sure to copy the data file to an alternate disk. And now this alter tablespace is called **end backup statement.** During activity database will open all the time and backup took place, and in this process administrator should archive redo logs that were collected during backup of database and executes **archive log list** statement to find which redo logs were used.

Test Your Progress

1. Why is security necessary in data warehousing?
2. Explain the types of backup and recovery methods of data warehouse.

7.10 Tuning and Testing of Data Warehouse:

Tuning the Data Warehouse

The data warehouse evolves throughout the time and it is unpredictable that what question user can create in future. So it becomes harder to tune data warehouse system. Data warehouse system is made up by multiple databases from multiple sources, so it becomes difficult to tune data warehouse system. There are various difficulties in data warehouse. Tuning is also defined:

*   The data warehouse varies time-to-time.
*   User's queries are unpredictable.
*   With time, need of the business will also be changed.
*   With respect to time users and their profile will change.
*   The user can switch from one group to another.
*   In the warehouse data load has to be changed with time.

It is designed for data availability and after recovery considerations. Data warehouse activity aim to provide data using Extract, Transform and Load (ETL), and Business Intelligence (BI).

During the ETL phase, data from operational systems is:

*   **Extracted** – This is the first phase, which will read data from operational database, basically it is unloaded data.
*   **Transformed** – Aim of the transformation is to convert the extracted data into needed form of database. This transformation can be done by combining the data and by using rules and lookup tables.
*   **Loaded** –Write the data in tables of the data warehouse.

During the BI (Business Intelligence) phase, variety of software has to be used to analyze organization's raw data; for example statistical analysis, customer support, customer profiling, market segmentation, product profitability, market research, and inventory and distribution analysis, etc.

Data warehouse design takes ETL and BI phases into account using two main strategies:

- **Table Partitioning:** At the time of table design, table should be partitioned on the basis of its dimension used.

- **Fact and Dimension Tables**: Dimension table contains selection criteria whereas fact tables contain aggregated or summarized data.

Tuning Queries

There are two kinds of queries in data warehouse: (i) Fixed Queries, (ii) Ad hoc Queries. Let us discuss each of them in brief.

- **Fixed Queries:** Fixed queries like regular reports, canned queries, aggregation are almost similar to relational database system. But here amount of data to be queried may vary.

- **Adhoc Queries:** Ad hoc queries are done by adhoc users; these users's nature is not predictable and show varying effect on individual user or group of users.

- Number of users in the group.

- Whether they use ad hoc queries frequently, in regular interval or occasionally.

- Number of queries in an peak hour.

- Size of query they run.

- Elapsed login time per day.

- Peak time of daily usage.

So when processed these queries remember those points because as the query becomes more adhoc, the job of tuning the data warehouse becomes difficult. To solve this problem adhoc queries should be tuned as predictable manner as adding new indexes and aggregations. This maintains the throughput and power of machine for complex adhoc queries.

Testing the Data Warehouse

Without testing the data warehouse could produce incorrect answer and quickly loss the faith of the users. A successful testing requires putting together the right process, people and technology and deploying them in productive ways.

There are basically three levels of testing that are listed below:

(i)   Unit Testing

(ii) Integration Testing

(iii) System Testing

(i)   Unit Testing

- In the unit testing, each module is tested individually.

- It is a kind of testing in which we can test different module like program, procedure, script etc

- This type of testing is done using software developer.

(ii) Integration Testing

- In this type of testing, all the modules are arranged together and after that tested through the various inputs.
- It is performed to test whether the various components do well after integration.

(iii) System Testing

- In this type of testing, we can test the whole application together.
- The goal of this testing is to identify whether the whole system will work correctly together or not.
- This type of testing is performed by the software tester.
- The size of whole data warehouse application become large, so it difficult to test the entire system.

Challenges of Data Warehouse Testing

- Data selection from multiple source and analysis that follows pose great challenge.
- Volume and complexity of the data.
- Redundant data in a data ware house.
- Inconsistent and inaccurate reports.

Test Your Progress

1. Explain the testing of data warehouse.
2. Discuss the tuning of data warehouse.

7.9   Summary:

In this chapter, we have learnt about Online Analytical Processing (OLAP) systems, contrary to the regular, conventional Online Transaction Processing (OLTP) systems, which are capable of analyzing online a large number of past transactions and summarize them on the fly. This chapter also discussed about OLAP tools, servers , their advantages and disadvantages, and tuning and testing of data warehouse.

7.10   Key Terms

- **Aggregation:** A technique to merge or consolidate dispersed data into a single data.
- **Backup:** The process of the copying and archiving of computer data so it may be used to restore the original after a data loss event.
- **OLAP:** OnLine Analytical Processing.
- **OLAP server:** A server provides functionality and performance that leverages the data warehouse for reporting, analysis, modeling and planning requirements.
- **QBE:** Query by Example; a database query language for relational databases.

7.11 Exercise

1. What is OLAP? Explain various OLAP operations used on a data cube.
2. Compare ROLAP and MOLAP.
3. Distinguish between OLTP system and OLAP system.
4. Give some advantages of OLAP systems.
5. Differentiate between ROLAP,MOLAP and HOLAP.
6. What is the need of aggregation in data warehousing?
7. Explain different types of index techniques.
8. What is a fixed and adhocquery.
9. Explain data warehouse security in detail.

University Questions

1. What is Aggregation? Explain.   **[UPTU 2009-10, 2010-11]**
   Refer section 7.1.2
2. Explain the Query facility providing by data warehouse.   **[UPTU 2008-09]**
   Refer Section 7.7
3. What is OLAP?   **[UPTU 2003-04, 2004-05, 2008-09]**
   Refer Section 7.1
4. Describe the functions and tools of OLAP.
                [UPTU 2003-04, 2008-09, 2009-10]
   Refer Section 7.2
5. Describe the following terms (i) ROLAP (ii) MOLAP (iii) HOLAP
            [UPTU 2005-06, 2008-09,2009-10, 2010-11, 2011-12,2013-14]
   Refer Section 7.4
6. Explain multidimensional data and data cube, explain operations performed on multidimensional data cube.   **[UPTU 2010-11]**
   Refer Section 7.1.1 and 7.2
7. Describe the MOLAP and ROLAP in brief. Write theircontribution in building of data warehouse.   **[UPTU 2010-11]**
   Refer Section 7.4.1 and 7.4.2
8. Tuning and testing Data Warehouse .
          [UPTU ,2009-2010 ,2010-11, 2011-12, 2012-13,2013-2014]
   Refer Section 7.10
9. SLICE and DICE operation   **[UPTU 2009-10]**
   Refer Section 7.2
10. Describe the various OLAP operations. Explain how query processing can be improved by cascading the operations.   **[UPTU 2011-12]**
    Refer Section 7.2

11. Differentiate between OLTP and OLAP.
    [UPTU 2006-07, 2007-08, 2008-09, 2009-10, 2010-2011, 2012-13, 2013-14]
    Refer Section 7.3

12. Describe the various types of OLAP Servers.   **[UPTU 2012-13]**
    Refer Section 7.4

13. Security issues in data warehouse   **[UPTU 2012-13]**
    Refer Section 7.9

14. Explain Backup and recovery of data warehouse   **[UPTU 2012-13,2013-14]**
    Refer Section 7.9

15. Explain data mining interface.   **[UPTU 2010-11, 2012-13, 2013-14]**
    Refer Section 7.8

Section B
Advanced Topic on Data Mining and Warehousing

8.1 Text Mining

The popular and increasing use of World Wide Web (WWW) has made the Web a rich and gigantic repository of information. A significant amount of the available information is stored in the form of text databases. These databases contain large collections of documents from diverse sources, such as books, research papers, new articles, digital libraries, e-mail messages and Web pages. These days most of the government, industrial, business and other organizations also store their information electronically, in the form of text databases.

Data stored in such databases is in semi-structured form, that is, neither completely unstructured nor completely structured. For example, a document may contain few structured fields, such as title, authors, category, data_of_publishing, etc., and may also contain some unstructured text components, such as abstract and contents. The process of deriving useful information and patterns from such databases is known is **text mining.** The traditional data mining techniques that focus on structured data cannot be used for text mining. Therefore, some sophisticated techniques are required for text mining. In recent database research, a great deal of studies on the modelling and implementation of semi-structured data have been carried out.

Since the information stored in text databases is increasing day-by-day, the traditional information retrieval techniques have become inadequate. Thus, several information techniques, such as text indexing methods, have been developed to handle increasingly vast amount of unstructured text data. Note that although a large number of docments are available, only a small fraction of documents will be relevant to a given individual user at any point of time. Thus, some sophisticated tools are also required which help the users to compare different documents, to rank their important and relevance, and to find patterns and trends across multiple documents. Therefore, text mining is gaining popularity in the field of data mining.

8.2 Information Retrieval

It refers to the process of organizing and extracting the information from a large number of text-based documents. That is, Information Retrieval (IR) extracts information from unstructured form of data. Since IR system and database systems handle different kinds of data, some database issues, such as recovery, concurrency control, update etc., are not encountered in IR system. Due to the abundance of text information, IR systems are gaining popularity these days. Many IR systems, such as online library catalog systems, online document management systems and the most popular Web search engines have been developed. The main challenge in an IR system task is to locate relevant information from numerous documents based on a user's query which is in the form of some keywords describing his/her need. If he/she has a short-term information need then he/she can take the initiative to 'pull' the useful information out from the collection, whereas if he/she has a long-term information need, then the retrieval system may also take initiative to 'push' any newly arrived information to desired user. Accessing information in such a manner is known as information filtering and the corresponding systems are called **filtering systems** or **recommender systems.** In general, there are two basic methods of retrieving the information from text-base databases, such as, **document selection method** and **document ranking method.** In document selection method query is considered as specifying constraints for selecting relevant documents whereas document ranking methods rank all the documents according to their relevance. That is, a user query is matched against the document collection to present a ranked list of documents on the basis of how well it matches the query.

8.3   Web Mining

A natural combination of the two areas data mining and World Wide Web (WWW) sometimes referred to as Web mining. Web mining is the application of data mining techniques to discover patterns from Web. There are some challenges that one needs to consider for extracting useful knowledge from such huge amount of data. These challenges are:

● Size of the Web is too large for effective data warehousing and data mining. This size is growing rapidly as many organizations load most of their information on the Web so that it can be easily accessed by everyone. Thus it is almost impossible to build a data warehouse which can store, replicate and integrate all of the Web data.

● The Web is considered a huge digital library containing a large number of traditional text-based documents. These documents lack a unifying structure. Moreover, they have different authoring styles and content variations and above all these documents are not arranged according to any particular sorted order.

● The Web is having a huge user community in which users may have different interests, backgrounds and usage purposes. Most of them are not even having knowledge of the structure of the information network and may also not be aware of the costs involved in performing a specific search. They cannot wait for long time for the page to get completely loaded or become irritated by not knowing the links which would help them in searching the required document.

● The Web servers tremendous information, but it is said that only a small portion of such information is relevant to the users. That is, 99% of the Web information is useless to 99% of Web users. This is laid because a particular user is interested only in that portion of information which is desirable to his query, while the rest of the Web data are unimportant and useless.

Web mining is divided into three different types which are Web usage mining, Web content mining and Web structure mining.

i. **Web Content Mining:** It is the process of extracting, integrating and mining useful knowledge and information from web page contents.

ii. **Web Usage Mining:** It is the process of extracting useful information on the basis of user log. That is, finding out the type of data user is looking for by examining the server logs.

iii. **Web Structure Mining:** It is the process of using graph theory to analyze the node and connection structure of website. This can be done either by extracting patterns from hyperlinks in the Web or by describing the Hyper Text Markup Language (HTML) or eXtensible Markup Language (XML) tags in the form of tree-like structures.

8.4 Spatial Data Mining

Spatial data mining is the process of extracting knowledge, spatial relationships or interesting patterns from a large set of spatial databases. Spatial data, such as maps, medical imaging data, remote sensing data, and layout of VLSI design, etc. it is a special data refers to that data which have a location or spatial component associated with it. Spatial data mining requires the integration of data mining with spatial databases technologies. Such mining can be used for understanding spatial data, discovering relationships between spatial and non-spatial data, constructing spatial knowledge bases, recognizing spatial databases and optimizing spatial queries. Due to the huge amount of spatial data and complexity of spatial data types and spatial access methods, spatial data mining requires efficient spatial data mining techniques. Spatial data mining can be used in various application areas, such as Geographical Information System (GIS), remote sensing, image database exploration, traffic control, navigation and so on.

Spatial statistical modelling methods are mostly used for analyzing spatial data and for exploring geographical information. The traditional statistical model which handles non-spatial data assumes statistical independence among different portions of data but, in spatial statistical model there is no such assumption made among spatial data as they are generally interrelated. That is they follow the property that more closely they are located, the more likely they share similar characteristics. This property of close interdependency among nearby located objects is known as spatial autocorrelation, which thus from the basis of developing effective spatial statistical data analysis methods.

8.5 Application of data warehousing and data mining in government sector

Government deals with huge amount of data and to ensure that such data are used effectively for decision making, two technologies, such as data warehousing and data mining are used in combination. These technologies are considered to be the important source of preparing the government for facing new challenges in the upcoming generation and can be effectively implemented in both central and state government sectors. Some of the potential applications in the government sector where these technologies can be used as follows:

1. **Agriculture:** The agriculture census performed by ministry of agriculture stores huge amount of agriculture parameters, such as district-wise agricultural production and yield of crops, data on agricultural inputs, data from livestock census and land-use pattern statistics. Such data can be built into a data warehouse for analysis, mining and forecasting by applying the technologies of OLAP and data mining. Thus, one can say that two technologies have broad scope in the agricultural sector.

2. **Rural Development:** Data warehousing and data mining technologies can be effectively implemented in the area of rural development. Data on individuals Below Poverty Line (BPL) and data based on drinking water census can be built into a data warehouse. Moreover, the growth in rural development programmes can also be checked, observed and analyzed using OLAP and data mining techniques.

3. **Health:** Various types of health-related data, such as immunization data, data from national programmes on controlling various diseases (such as leprosy, blindness), assessment data, etc., can all be used for data warehousing implementation, OLAP and data mining applications.

4. **Education:** The data of the sixth All India Educational Survey were converted into a data warehouse from which several different analytical queries can be answered and numerous reports can be handle.

5. **Planning:** In this area, data from various sectors, such as labour, energy, trade, five year plan, etc., can be built into a data warehouse. This helps in accumulating all data for particular state at one place which thus provides effective planning which needs to be made for the growth of the state.

6. **Commerce and Trade**: Here, data available with the Ministry of Commerce can be analyzed and converted into a data warehouse. Moreover, world price monitoring system can be made to perform better by making use of data warehousing and data mining technologies. Furthermore, tentative estimates of import and export can be made more accurate using various forecasting techniques.

7. **Others**: There are several other application areas where data warehousing and data mining can be very useful. Such potential application areas include tourism, revenue, economic affairs, audit and accounts etc.

8.6   Statistical Data Mining

Most of the data mining techniques are designed to handle multidimensional and other complex types of data. There are various well established statistical techniques which are designed for analysis and efficient handling of numeric data. These techniques can be applied to scientific data, such as in physics, medicine, psychology, etc., and also to data of economic and social sciences. Some technologies, such as regression, PCA and clustering have already been discussed in previous Chapters, but several other methods which can handle numeric data are also there. These are generalized linear models, mixed-effect models, factor analysis, survival analysis, etc.

8.7 Visual Data Mining

It discovers implicit and useful knowledge from large datasets using data and/ or knowledge visualization techniques. It is a highly attractive and effective tool for understanding the patterns, clusters and outliers in data and is also closely associated with computer graphics, pattern recognition, multimedia systems and human-computer interaction. Visual data mining is formed from the integration of two components, such as data visualization and data mining. This integration can be done in the following ways:

- **Data visualization:** As data in data warehouse or database can be viewed at different levels of abstraction or as different combination of dimensions, a visual display helps a user to give a clear presentation and overview of the data characteristics in such repositories. Various visual forms in which such data can be effectively presented are 3D cubes, data distribution charts, curves, link graphs, etc.

- **Data mining result visualization:** It is the presentation of the result or knowledge obtained from data mining in visual forms. Such visual forms may include scatter plots, boxplots, association rules, outliers, clusters, etc.

- **Data mining process visualization:** Here, a complete data mining process is presented in visual forms so that users can easily understand the several sub-processes occurring in such system. That is, it tells a user clearly about the method chosen for data mining; how data are extracted from database or data warehouse; how the selected data are cleaned, integrated, preprocessed and mined; where the results are stored and how they can be viewed.

- **Interactive visual data mining:** Here, visualization tools can be used in data mining process to help users in making better data mining decisions. For example, the set of attributes of the dataset can be displayed among several sectors of different colours within a circle. This distribution will help users to determine which sectors should be first selected for classification and where a good split point for this sector may be.

8.8 Constraint-based Cluster Analysis

It is sometimes desirable to consider user preferences and constraints while performing cluster analysis. Such constraints include the expected number of clusters, the minimal and maximal cluster size, weights for different objects or dimensions and other desirable characteristics of the resulting clusters. This will lead to more desirable results as knowledge discovery from such type of clusters will be more meaningful. Therefore, it can be said that constraint-based clustering is a technique which finds clusters on the basis of the constraints specified by users. Depending on the nature of the constraints, this technique adopts the following approaches:

1. **Constraints on individual object:** In this approach, one specifies constraints on the objects which are to be clustered. For example, in a real estate application, one may only like to cluster those luxury mansions whose worth is over 1000 dollars. It can be handled easily by pre-processing, after which the problem reduces to an instance of the unconstrained clustering.

2. **Constraints on the selection of clustering parameters**: in this approach clustering parameters can be set to the desired range as desired by the user. These parameters are quite specific to a given clustering algorithm and are usually confined to the algorithm itself. Therefore, their fine tuning and processing are usually not considered a form of constrained-based clustering.

3. **Constraints on distance or similarity functions:** In this approach, a user may specify different distance or similarity functions for specific attributes of objects, or different distance measures for specific pairs of objects which are to be clustered.

4. **User-specified constraints on the properties of individual clusters**: In this approach, a user may specify desired characteristics of the resulting clusters, which may strongly influence the clustering process.

5. **Semi-supervised clustering based on partial supervision:** In this approach, the quality of unsupervised clustering is improved by using some weak form of supervision. This may be done in the form of pair wise constraints in which pairs of objects labelled as belonging to the same or different clusters. Such a clustering process based on user feedback or guidance constraints is called semi-supervised clustering.

8.9 Big Data : Data Analytics

Big data is a new concept, comes in reality as 3V: **Volume, Variety** and **Velocity** of data coming in to network communication medium from one organization to another organization or from one computer to another computer. Big data is used in order to decipher the information that truly count, but you must be exactly know what you can do in big data analytics.

What is Big Data Analytics?

Big data analytics is the process of investigative big data to uncover hidden pattern, unknown correlation and other useful information that can be used to make better decisions. With big data analytics, data scientists and others can analyze vast volumes of data that conservative analytics and business intelligence solutions cannot touch. Consider this; it is possible that your organization could accumulate (if it hasn't already) billions of rows of data with hundreds of millions of data combinations in multiple data stores and abundant formats. High-performance analytics is necessary to process that much data in order to figure out what is important and what is not. Enter big data analytics.

Why collect and store terabytes of data if you cannot analyze it in full context? Or if you have to wait hours or days to get results? With new advances in computing technology, there is no need to avoid tackling even the most difficult and challenging business problems. For simpler and faster processing of only relevant data, you can use high-performance analytics. Using high-performance data mining, predictive analytics, text mining, forecasting and optimization on big data enables you to continuously drive innovation and make the best possible decisions. In addition, organizations are discovering that the unique properties of machine learning are ideally suited to addressing their fast-paced big data needs in new ways.

www.ingramcontent.com/pod-product-compliance
Lightning Source LLC
Chambersburg PA
CBHW071219050326
40689CB00011B/2370